NRAEF ManageFirst
Inventory and Purchasing
Competency Guide

PEARSON
Prentice
Hall

Upper Saddle River, New Jersey 07458

Disclaimer

Table of Contents

i

A Message from the National Restaurant Association Educational Foundation

The National Restaurant Association Educational Foundation (NRAEF) is a not-for-profit organization dedicated to fulfilling the educational mission of the National Restaurant Association. We focus on helping the restaurant and foodservice industry address its risk management, recruitment, and retention challenges.

As the nation's largest private-sector employer, the restaurant, hospitality, and foodservice industry is the cornerstone of the American economy, of career-and-employment opportunities, and of local communities. The total economic impact of the restaurant industry is astounding—representing approximately 10 percent of the U.S. gross domestic product. At the NRAEF, we are focused on enhancing this position by providing the valuable tools and resources needed to educate our current and future professionals.

For more information on the NRAEF, please visit our Web site at *www.nraef.org.*

What is the NRAEF ManageFirst Program?

The NRAEF ManageFirst Program is a management-training certificate program that exemplifies our commitment to developing materials by the industry, for the industry. The program's most powerful strength is that it is based on a set of competencies defined by the restaurant, foodservice, and hospitality industry as critical for success.

NRAEF ManageFirst Program Components

The NRAEF ManageFirst Program includes a set of competency guides, exams, instructor resources, certificates, a new credential, and support activities and services. By participating in the program, you are demonstrating your commitment to becoming a highly qualified professional either preparing to begin or to advance your career in the restaurant, hospitality, and foodservice industry.

The competency guides cover the range of topics listed in the chart at right.

Competency Guide/Exam Topics

NRAEF ManageFirst Core Credential Topics

Hospitality and Restaurant Management

Controlling Foodservice Costs

Human Resources Management and Supervision

ServSafe® Food Safety

NRAEF ManageFirst Foundation Topics

Managerial Accounting

Inventory and Purchasing

Customer Service

Food Production

Menu Marketing and Management

Restaurant Marketing

Nutrition

ServSafe Alcohol™ Responsible Alcohol Service

Within the guides, you will find the essential content for the topic as defined by industry, as well as learning activities, assessments, case studies, suggested field projects, professional profiles, and testimonials. You will also find an answer sheet for an NRAEF exam written specifically for each topic. The exam can be administered either online or in a paper and pencil format, and it will be proctored. Upon successfully passing the exam, you will be furnished by the NRAEF with a customized certificate. The certificate is a lasting recognition of your accomplishment and a signal to the industry that you have mastered the competency covered within the particular topic.

To earn the NRAEF's new credential, you will be required to pass four core exams and one foundation exam (to be chosen from the remaining program topics) and to document your work experience in the restaurant and foodservice industry. Earning the NRAEF credential is a significant accomplishment.

We applaud you as you either begin or advance your career in the restaurant, hospitality, and foodservice industry. Visit *www.nraef.org* to learn about additional career-building resources offered by the NRAEF, including scholarships for college students enrolled in relevant industry programs.

NRAEF ManageFirst Program Ordering Information

Review copies or support materials:
FACULTY FIELD SERVICES
Tel: 800.526.0485

Domestic orders and inquiries:
PEARSON CUSTOMER SERVICE
Tel: 800.922.0579
www.prenhall.com

International orders and inquiries:
U.S. EXPORT SALES OFFICE
Pearson Education International Customer Service Group
200 Old Tappan Road
Old Tappan, NJ 07675 USA
Tel: 201.767.5021
Fax: 201.767.5625

For corporate, government and special sales (consultants, corporations, training centers, VARs, and corporate resellers) orders and inquiries:
PEARSON CORPORATE SALES
Tel: 317.428.3411
Fax: 317.428.3343
Email: managefirst@prenhall.com

For additional information regarding other Prentice Hall publications, instructor and student support materials, locating your sales representative and much more, please visit *www.prenhall.com/managefirst.*

Acknowledgements

The National Restaurant Association Educational Foundation is grateful for the expertise and guidance of our many advisors, subject matter experts, reviewers, and other contributors.

We are pleased to thank the following people for their time, effort, and dedication to this program.

Ernest Boger

Robert Bosselman

Jerald Chesser

Cynthia Deale

Fred DeMicco

John Drysdale

Gene Fritz

John Gescheidle

Thomas Hamilton

John Hart

Thomas Kaltenecker

Ray Kavanaugh

John Kidwell

Carol Kizer

Cynthia Mayo

Fred Mayo

Patrick Moreo

Robert O'Halloran

Brian O'Malley

Terrence Pappas

James Perry

William N. Reynolds

Rosenthal Group

Mokie Steiskal

Karl Titz

Terry Umbreit

Deanne Williams

Mike Zema

Features of the NRAEF ManageFirst Competency Guides

We have designed the NRAEF ManageFirst Competency Guides to enhance your ability to learn and retain important information that is critical to this restaurant and foodservice industry function. Here are the key features you will find within this guide.

Beginning Each Guide

Tuning In to You

When you open an NRAEF ManageFirst Competency Guide for the first time, you might ask yourself: Why do I need to know about this topic? Every topic of these guides involves key information you will need as you manage a restaurant or foodservice operation. Located in the front of each review guide, "Tuning In to You" is a brief synopsis that illustrates some of the reasons the information contained throughout that particular guide is important to you. It exemplifies real-life scenarios that you will face as a manager and how the concepts in the book will help you in your career.

Professional Profile

This is your opportunity to meet a professional who is currently working in the field associated with a competency guide's topic. This person's story will help you gain insight into the responsibilities related to his or her position, as well as the training and educational history linked to it. You will also see the daily and cumulative impact this position has on an operation, and receive advice from a person who has successfully met the challenges of being a manager.

Beginning Each Chapter

Inside This Chapter

Chapter content is organized under these major headings.

Learning Objectives

Learning objectives identify what you should be able to do after completing each chapter. These objectives are linked to the required tasks a manager must be able to perform in relation to the function discussed in the competency guide.

Test Your Knowledge

Each chapter begins with some True or False questions designed to test your prior knowledge of some of the concepts presented in the chapter. The answers to these questions, as well as the concepts behind them, can be found within the chapter—see the page reference after each question.

Key Terms

These terms are important for thorough understanding of the chapter's content. They are highlighted throughout the chapter, where they are explicitly defined or their meaning is made clear within the paragraphs in which they appear.

Throughout Each Chapter

Exhibits

Exhibits are placed throughout each chapter to visually reinforce the key concepts presented in the text. Types of exhibits include charts, tables, photographs, and illustrations.

Think About It...

These thought-provoking sidebars reveal supportive information about the section they appear beside.

Activities

Apply what you have learned throughout the chapter by completing the various activities in the text. The activities have been designed to give you additional practice and better understanding of the concepts addressed in the learning objectives. Types of activities include case studies, role-plays, and problem solving, among others.

Exhibit

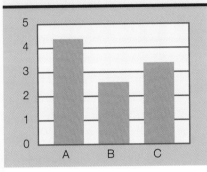

Exhibits are visuals that will help you learn about key concepts.

Think About It...

Consider these supplemental insights as you read through a chapter.

Activity

Activity

Types of activities you will complete include case studies, role-plays, and problem solving, among others.

At the End of Each Chapter

Review Your Learning

These multiple-choice or open- or close-ended questions or problems are designed to test your knowledge of the concepts presented in the chapter. These questions have been aligned with the objectives and should provide you with an opportunity to practice or apply the content that supports these objectives. If you have difficulty answering them, you should review the content further.

At the End of the Guide

Field Project

This real-world project gives you the valuable opportunity to apply many of the concepts you will learn in a competency guide. You will interact with industry practitioners, enhance your knowledge, and research, apply, analyze, evaluate, and report on your findings. It will provide you with an in-depth "reality check" of the policies and practices of this management function.

Tuning In to You

One thing that all restaurant and foodservice operations have in common is that they must purchase goods and services. It is important that these goods are selected in such a way that the operation will have an adequate supply on hand for sale, and that the goods meet the operation's established quality requirements. If you oversee the purchasing duties of an operation, you will need a wide field of knowledge about suppliers, goods, and services. You will be buying everything from meat, poultry, produce, and alcoholic and non-alcoholic beverages, to nonfood items such as dinnerware, silverware, candles, linens, and cleaning supplies. The purchasing function also includes administrative work and keeping good relationships with suppliers. Failure to handle all these duties correctly can lead to budget difficulties, and employee and customer dissatisfaction.

The exact job description of a purchaser is usually shaped by the specific operation's policies and needs, and should include duties that relate to these skill sets. For example, an owner might be responsible for purchasing food items, while the bar manager might be responsible for beverage purchasing. There are ethical considerations to keep in mind as well, and the rules and guidelines concerning ethics in purchasing exist to protect all parties involved.

Purchasers are also responsible for establishing quality standards for the products in your operation. Additionally, choosing the appropriate buyers and suppliers is an integral part of any operation, and a purchaser needs to be careful when making these decisions, being sure to select a supplier who can fully accommodate the operation. For example, you would not want to choose a supplier who does not comply with local, state, and federal laws, or one who does not have sufficient holding units to maintain the temperature needed for refrigerated or frozen storage.

The purchasing function does not end once products or services are bought. Ideally, restaurant or foodservice establishments strive to keep on hand only the needed quantity of food and nonfood products to meet customer needs—without experiencing stock outs—but not more inventory than needed. The process of managing inventory goes hand in hand with buying an operation's products and services, and the process varies greatly among establishments, with some operations using theoretical counts of inventory and others using physical (actual) counting of inventory. In all cases, you will need to manage inventory procedures in order to manage the entire purchasing function effectively.

Professional Profile
Your opportunity to meet someone working in the field

Hal Axelrod

Club House Manager
Skokie Country Club
Skokie, IL

Like many job titles, mine does not clearly reflect all of the varied purchasing and inventory tasks I perform on a daily basis. I am the Club House Manager at the Skokie Country Club, a private golf club in a northern suburb of Chicago, Illinois.

In my role, I oversee all food and beverage operations, which generate over two million dollars in revenue. I assist in hiring all front-of-the-house food and beverage staff and coordinate the continuing education of all staff and the training for all newly hired staff. I am responsible for ordering all beverages—from soda to fine wines—and for purchasing china, glass, silverware, and other dining service items.

When I am not devoting my time to working in the dining rooms, you can find me coordinating the operation's purchasing function and service with my team of three assistant managers and fifty food and beverage employees.

I have worked in the restaurant and foodservice industry for thirty years, and I've come a long way in that time. My first job was scraping plates at a restaurant in the Union at the University of Illinois. Who knew that a job I took to pay the bills during my freshman year at school would turn out to be the start of a career in the hospitality industry? I was attending school to become a teacher and actually taught for two and a half years in two different public schools. However, to supplement my income, I always turned to the hospitality industry for jobs. I used my experience as a plate scraper to get a job as a waiter, which led to a variety of jobs, including bartending and a banquet captain.

I gave up my teaching career and took my first management position with Morton Management. After six years at Morton's, I went to work for The Levy Restaurants at three different locations in downtown Chicago. I then owned and operated a pasta concept called Dancing Noodles Café, wearing many hats, including that of a buyer. After seven years, I sold the restaurant and spent two years as the Director of Education for the Illinois Restaurant Association. Since that job, my attention has been focused on private club management.

Starting with my earliest job as a manager, I was thrust into the role of a purchaser who directly bought items for the operation or supervised others who also procured goods or services. I realized very early that even at the most basic level, a checks and balance system was essential to ensure that proper selection, purchasing, receiving, storing, and issuing of items was performed.

While working in a large operation, I was told from which suppliers I could buy my operation's products. However, I had the responsibility of determining whether these suppliers provided the operation with the best prices. I regularly compared their prices to those of other similar vendors for the same products. In doing this, I realized that while pricing is very important, there is more to getting the best overall value than exclusively considering just the cost of an item—and that's the relationships you develop with the purveyors and the services they offer.

I saw firsthand how many supplier sources bent over backward to win over my operation or other operations with which they sought to do business. Even large operations that seemingly have very little flexibility look for suppliers who offer services like free delivery or discounts, which allow them to gain the greatest overall value and transfer low-cost specials in food and beverage to their customers.

While I have formed relationships with vendors through conversations that were held over the telephone, I prefer to establish them in person. I feel it is important to speak face-to-face with sales staff or owners, as this allows me to gain a better sense of the people with whom I'm building a very important relationship. Too, it's always fun to match a face with a voice.

Working with a supplier or a sales person is as vital as working with any partner. Just as you desire open communication, honesty, trust, and affability in any important relationship, as a buyer, you seek the same with your supplier(s). Working with a supplier who works with you and who has your operation's best interests in mind is critical. I expect that the suppliers with whom I work show me new items or let me know when prices might spike higher or dip lower. I try to use multiple vendors and frequently compare pricing, which often keeps them even more honest. This is harder to do with the beverage side, given that there is typically one vendor for each product.

Before selecting any vendor, I communicate with many. While the first vendor with whom I speak may be the one I ultimately select, it is not the only or last one I interview. To make certain that any supplier or salesperson is somebody with whom I will do business or that completely complies with my operation's standards, I also visit their sites and check out their storage facilities, including temporary ones, like their delivery trucks. Looking at suppliers' businesses during hours of operation and meeting the people behind the scenes give me a sense of the character of the organization and its people.

How you go about performing the purchasing function for your operation can make or break it. Beyond the impact that the type of products you select and from whom you purchase them have on the operation, your actions greatly impact the operation's finances. You must be aware of how your decisions impact the operation's bottom line. For example, if you are paying more for food and beverage items than you had budgeted, one of two things will follow: you will either raise your menu prices accordingly or your operation's costs will increase and its profits will decrease. The latter does not bode well for the operation or for you.

Once an item is purchased, your inventory should reflect this as well as any price change. Taking inventory on a daily, weekly, or monthly schedule is critical. It allows you to know when, what, and how much to order; you never want to have to tell a customer that you are out of something. Maintaining an inventory also helps you to secure control over the products you purchase. It is a mechanism that serves to decrease the chance of product loss owing to theft or pilferage or product spoilage. It also figures into the operation's percentage costs. Taking daily inventories of some items can also alert you to product waste.

Every experience I have had and every title I have held have contributed to my knowledge of purchasing and inventory. So with that said, know that whether you start out as a food scraper, a server, a short-order cook, a sous chef, or a bartender, the relationships you make at any operation may last a career.

Introduction to Inventory and Purchasing

1

Inside This Chapter
- The Objectives of Purchasing
- What to Buy

After completing this chapter, you should be able to:
- Define purchasing, procurement, and product selection.
- Outline the objectives in the purchasing function.
- Describe the importance of maintaining an operation's competitive position.
- List the types of goods and services that might be purchased by a foodservice organization.

Test Your Knowledge

1. **True or False:** The goal of purchasing is to obtain the lowest possible as purchased (AP) price. *(See p. 4.)*

2. **True or False:** Customer count forecasts and vendor delivery schedules are the only tools for ensuring that an adequate supply of product is available for sale. *(See p. 4.)*

3. **True or False:** Items should be purchased in large quantities to minimize time spent ordering. *(See p. 6.)*

4. **True or False:** Foodservice buyers compete against each other to obtain the best prices for goods and services. *(See p. 7.)*

5. **True or False:** Foodservice operations are both manufacturers and retailers; therefore, they do not have to purchase a wide array of products and services. *(See p. 9.)*

Key Terms

As purchased (AP) price

As served (AS) price

Cash position

Competitive advantage

Cooperative or Co-op buying

Covers

Customer count history

Economies of scale

Edible portion (EP) price

Franchise

Popularity index

Procurement

Product selection

Profit

Purchasing

Vendor

Think About It...

From where would a large, national chain purchase its goods and services? Why?

Introduction

Whether a small neighborhood bistro, an employee cafeteria, or a national chain, all restaurants and foodservice establishments must purchase goods and services. Relatively few foodservice operations, however, are able to employ professional buyers. Therefore, products are often selected and ordered by personnel whose responsibilities and expertise lie in areas such as food production, service management, and office management.

Goods and services must be selected and procured in such a way that the operation has an adequate supply on hand for sale. They must meet established quality guidelines. Products and services must be purchased in a manner that minimizes the operation's capital investment. Obtaining prices equal to or lower than that of competitors can greatly enhance an operation's competitive position. Considering the wide variety of products that must be purchased, purchasers must possess a wide field of knowledge. In this chapter, you will consider the primary objectives of purchasing and the range of goods and services purchased in the foodservice industry. *Exhibit 1a* below illustrates the purchasing function.

Exhibit 1a

Example of the Purchasing Function

Daniel Rizzano learned purchasing in a few ways. He learned it from his dad, who owns a franchise— a business that an independent owner buys from a company, along with the right to use the company's name, logo, and products. Daniel also learned the purchasing function while wearing just about all the hats in his own restaurant. He is the owner-manager-chef and buyer of his independent foodservice operation, Daniello's Ristorante, which is a neighbor to several other quaint *cucinas Italiano*.

He is solely responsible for purchasing—obtaining products and services of a desired quality at a desired price. Purchasing goods and services is much more than just buying them. Daniel must always be conscious of the true value of the items he is purchasing or procuring. Procurement is the entire process by which products and services are selected based upon quality and cost. This includes determining what goods and services will be needed, when they will be needed, and from what vendors—the companies that sell goods and services—as well as purchasing, receiving, and storing all the goods and services and managing the purchasing contracts.

During product selection—the process by which products and services are chosen based upon quality and cost—Daniel is conscious of what his neighbors' needs are. A few years ago, Daniel and some of the owner-managers of the other independent Italian restaurants in his area began combining their orders and cooperatively purchasing all their goods and services as a collective, in order to get lower prices from their suppliers. This is called cooperative buying or co-op buying. Daniel's dad, on the other hand, can choose to purchase his goods and services from his franchisor's central commissary and/or central distribution center. He can also purchase through a corporate-approved supplier that meets the franchisor's standards. This would allow him to take advantage of economies of scale—the savings that a multiunit business generates for itself by sharing the cost of purchasing goods and services.

While Daniel must select and procure all his goods and services in such a way as to ensure that he always has an adequate supply of quality goods and services for sale, he must also be careful to purchase them in a manner that minimizes his operation's capital investment. He must purchase a wide variety of products and services so his operation produces a profit—money received after all operating expenses have been paid.

Exhibit 1b

Goals of the Purchasing Function

1. Maintain adequate supply.

2. Maintain quality standards.

3. Minimize investment.

4. Maintain an operation's competitive position.

5. Obtain the lowest possible edible portion (EP) or as served (AS) price.

The Objectives of Purchasing

The primary objectives of the purchasing function are to maintain an adequate supply of products and services, maintain the quality standards established by a foodservice operation, minimize the operation's investment, maintain the operation's competitive position, and obtain the lowest possible edible portion (EP) or as served (AS) price, in order to contribute to the overall success of a foodservice operation. (See *Exhibit 1b*.)

Purchasing has a direct impact on the following:

- Availability of items for sale

- Type and quality of the operation's products

- Available funds an operation has on hand

- Profitability and competitive position of an operation

1. Maintain Adequate Supply

There are fewer things more disappointing to diners than ordering an item only to be told, "I'm sorry. We're out of that right now." The first goal of purchasing is to ensure that an adequate supply of product is available for sale. This is accomplished through a number of tools:

- Customer count histories

- Popularity index of items sold

- Vendor delivery schedules

- Availability of items from vendors

- Analysis of outside influences that might affect an operation, such as conventions, festivals, and weather forecasts

Astute purchasers will look at the operation's **customer count history** for clues in forecasting the number of customers an operation might serve, also known as **covers,** in a given period. For example, the number of customers served during the month of March last year will give an indication of the number of customers that might be served this March.

Additionally, nearby hotel occupancy, area conventions, and forecasts of upcoming inclement weather will help purchasers determine possible increases or decreases in sales. They must also know whether a particular item will be available in the market, as well as whether a vendor can deliver it when needed.

Exhibit 1c

Customers expect the same quality product each visit.

2. Maintain Quality Standards

Each item an operation produces must meet its standards for quality. A guest who enjoyed the "Kipper Burger" last week expects the same "Kipper Burger" this week. (See *Exhibit 1c.*) Substituting ground beef of an inferior grade will directly impact this customer's experience and satisfaction. Ensuring that the operation maintains consistent quality is another objective of purchasing and begins with buying products of a consistent quality. Maintaining quality standards can be more easily achieved by:

- Following the operation's established quality standards for each item or service when purchasing

- Clearly communicating these standards to potential vendors

These guidelines, as set by the chef, manager, and/or owner, are easy to follow when purchasing brand-name items, such as alcohol or condiments. Fresh food, however, presents challenges (to be discussed in Chapter 4). Freshness, seasonality, and availability make maintaining quality a challenge.

3. Minimize Investment

If purchasers were allocated unlimited funds to buy unlimited amounts of goods at any given time, the purchasing function would be greatly simplified. The reality is that an operation's funds are limited, and purchasers must carefully weigh the value of a potential purchase to an operation against the operation's **cash position—** the amount of funds available to it at any given time. Minimizing an operation's investment is another objective of purchasing.

Tying up large amounts of capital in products that will produce profit at a date far in the future can cripple a foodservice facility's ability to operate. Buying too much product can be as damaging as buying too little.

In order to minimize an operation's investment, consider the following:

- **Customer count forecast**

- **Anticipated cash needs for a given period**

- **Availability of storage for products**—Facilities possess limited storage space. Although additional storage may sometimes be purchased, this expense adds to the overall cost of items.

- **The forecasted future costs of items purchased**—Prices for many food items fluctuate greatly depending upon the season and weather conditions. It is sometimes cost effective to buy larger quantities of certain items "in season" while their prices are lower. Over time, however, prices rarely fall.

4. Maintain an Operation's Competitive Position

When you think of making a major consumer purchase—for example, a television—you might first determine the screen size you want. Next, you might decide on the characteristics and features you desire. You might even have a particular brand in mind. Once you have made these decisions, you might narrow your choices to a particular model. In the end, you will shop around for the best price and service available.

Foodservice purchasers operate similarly, except that they must also compete against one another for the best prices for goods and services, in order to obtain a **competitive advantage,** or position in relation to other restaurants. Maintaining a competitive advantage is another objective of purchasing. If Restaurant A can get better pricing and/or services than Restaurant B for similar items, Restaurant A will have a competitive advantage.

Although simple in concept, achieving this advantage in practice is difficult. Competitors rarely disclose their costs, and vendors often apply pricing levels unevenly among establishments by giving larger, higher-volume clients an advantage in pricing and added services.

To obtain this advantage, purchasers must do the following:

■ Choose vendors who will provide the best combination of price and service for their operational needs. Vendors sell more than products. They sell their services—frequency of delivery, emergency and odd-hour deliveries, flexible payment terms, low minimum orders, and consistency. Some larger vendors also include added services such as menu printing, free samples, and consulting services. Although the criteria for choosing vendors will be discussed more fully in Chapter 4, the idea of shopping around for the best prices and services cannot be emphasized enough.

■ Within the context of the operation's quality standards, concentrate on obtaining the lowest possible **edible portion (EP)** price—the cost of an item after all trimming and fabrication but before cooking, or **as served (AS)** price—the cost of an item as it is served to the customer. Obtaining the lowest possible EP or AS price is another objective of purchasing and will be discussed in the next section.

5. Obtain the Lowest Possible EP or AS Price

Operations must focus on the true cost of each item as it is served, not the **as purchased (AP) price,** which is the price of an item before all trimming, fabrication, and cooking. The AP price is too often considered the pertinent price. Cutting loss, labor costs during fabrication, and cooking loss contribute to a menu item's true cost. Obtaining the best EP or AS price is another objective of purchasing. This concept will be discussed further in Chapter 4.

The Consequences of Mismanaging the Purchasing Function

Mismanaging any of the primary objectives of the purchasing function can create situations that negatively impact your operation. Failure to maintain adequate supply of product can create product outages, which can lead to lost sales and dissatisfied customers. Failure to maintain quality standards can result in purchasing goods and services that do not meet the operation's quality standards or the quality that customers have come to expect from your operation. Although customers might forgive the occasional inconsistency, consistent inconsistency will lead to a loss of customers.

Purchasing too much product—overpurchasing—can tie up too much of the operation's capital and leave the operation with insufficient working cash. Likewise, paying too much for product and services affects working cash by increasing the operation's costs and thereby decreasing its profits. Insufficient working cash means that less cash is available to pay bills and for other projects, such as upgrading kitchen equipment or expanding the dining room.

Activity

Profit and Competitive Position

Il Pescatore is an Italian restaurant known for its Shrimp Scampi. The restaurant sold 2,100 orders of Shrimp Scampi last month and paid the current market average of $7.99 per pound for the Individually Quick Frozen (IQF) peeled and deveined shrimp used in the dish. Each portion requires six ounces of shrimp. Anna, the restaurant's purchasing agent, has found that she can exclusively obtain shrimp of comparable quality for $6.99 per pound for the next month by purchasing from another vendor.

Assuming the market price of frozen shrimp remains stable and the restaurant sells the same number of Shrimp Scampi this month as it did last month, how much will Anna's purchase contribute to the operation's profit, and thus to its competitive position?

To help determine the answer, calculate the following:

1. What are the total pounds of shrimp used?　＿＿＿＿＿＿＿＿＿＿

2. What is the new cost of the shrimp?　＿＿＿＿＿＿＿＿＿＿

3. What is the total savings that will contribute to the operation's profit, and thus to its competitive position?　＿＿＿＿＿＿＿＿＿＿

Think About It...

What other items might be included in the product and service categories?

What to Buy

Restaurants and foodservice operations are unusual within the business world because they are both manufacturer and retailer. This requires operations to purchase a wide array of products and services. Generally, these items are divided into categories. *Exhibit 1d* provides you with a brief look at these categories and some of the items they might include. Duplications occur within several categories because the item may be purchased outright or contracted as a service. For example, a restaurant could purchase linen or contract a linen service to provide it.

Exhibit 1d

Product and Service Categories

Food and Beverage

These are the items restaurants and foodservice operations actually prepare and sell. Examples include:

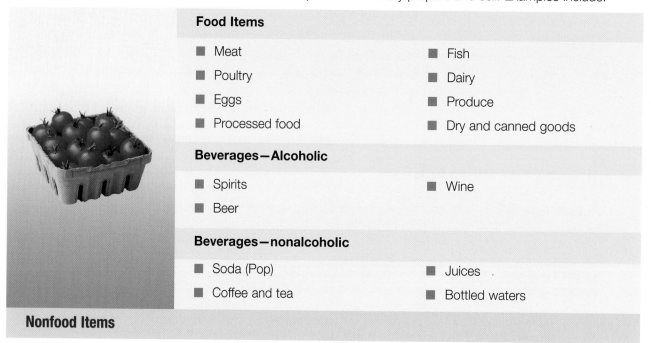

Food Items

- Meat
- Poultry
- Eggs
- Processed food
- Fish
- Dairy
- Produce
- Dry and canned goods

Beverages—Alcoholic

- Spirits
- Beer
- Wine

Beverages—nonalcoholic

- Soda (Pop)
- Coffee and tea
- Juices
- Bottled waters

Nonfood Items

These items are directly tied to the sale of food and beverages. For example, linen, candles, and flowers are used for tabletops, and paper bags are used for take-out orders. Other examples include:

- Linen and uniforms
- China and glassware
- Silverware
- Bar supplies
- Paper goods
- Cleaning supplies
- Menus and beverage lists
- Candles
- Flowers
- Music
- Kitchen utensils and supplies

Furniture, Fixtures, and Equipment

This category is also known as FFE or capital expenditures. Some of the items in this category may be purchased or leased, as is often the case with warewashing machines, ice machines, and beverage dispensing equipment. These "big ticket" appliances require significant maintenance and expensive repair. To reduce up-front capital expenses (especially during the start-up phase) and future maintenance and repair costs, many operations choose to lease these items rather than buy them.

Other examples of furniture, fixtures, and equipment include:

- Tables, chairs, and barstools
- Lighting fixtures
- Bars
- Cooking equipment
- Refrigeration
- Plumbing fixtures
- HVAC

Business Supplies and Services

These services and supplies are required for the management or marketing of the operation:

- Office supplies and equipment
- Cash registers and point-of-sale (POS) systems
- Computers
- Credit card processing
- Financial and legal services
- Insurance
- Marketing and advertising

Support Services

These support services are tied to the operational aspect of the business:

- Linen and uniform rental
- Waste removal
- Flower services
- Music services
- Pest control
- Parking and valet services

Maintenance Services

Maintenance services are required for the upkeep of the facility. These may include:

- Cleaning services
- Plumbing and heating
- Groundskeeping
- Painting and carpentry
- Equipment repair and maintenance

Utilities

In many areas of the country, businesses can choose among competing utility suppliers. Facilities may obtain significant savings by carefully selecting the following utility suppliers:

- Gas
- Oil heating
- Electricity
- Telephone service
- Internet access

Range image courtesy of Hobart Corporation

Summary

The purchasing function occupies an important role within the restaurant or foodservice industry and greatly contributes to a restaurant or foodservice operation's bottom line. A purchaser must ensure that an adequate supply of product is available for sale to customers, the product is consistently at the desired quality, the operation is investing a minimal amount of its available cash, and the product is obtained at or below the price that competitors are paying.

Failing to meet these objectives can damage the operation's reputation, limit the business' ability to meet its future financial obligations, reduce an operation's profitability, and put it at a competitive disadvantage.

A restaurant or foodservice operation must purchase a wide variety of goods and services in order to operate. Examples include food, beverages, equipment, and services, some of which could be either purchased or leased.

Review Your Learning

1 Which of these is an objective or goal in purchasing?

A. Obtaining the lowest possible AP price

B. Balancing the tradeoff between quality and price

C. Ordering in a way that ensures an adequate supply of product is on hand

D. Leasing equipment

2 Why is it important to minimize an operation's investment?

A. To maintain adequate cash reserves

B. To minimize storage costs

C. To ensure continued operation

D. All of the above

3 When comparing prices among vendors, buyers must focus on

A. EP price.

B. AP price.

C. the quantity available.

D. the weather forecast.

4 Which of these items is frequently leased rather than purchased outright?

A. Ranges

B. Warewashing machines

C. Tables and chairs

D. Paper goods

5 Those charged with purchasing must

A. possess a wide field of knowledge.

B. purchase food of specific quality.

C. avoid purchasing too much product.

D. All of the above

Notes

The Purchasing Function

2

Inside This Chapter

- ■ Purchasing in a Foodservice Operation
- ■ How Purchasing Affects an Operation's Employees
- ■ The Purchaser's Qualifications and Job Duties
- ■ Ethical Considerations Related to Purchasing
- ■ The Administration of Purchasing Activities

After completing this chapter, you should be able to:

- ■ Describe how the purchasing function is organized in a foodservice operation.
- ■ Summarize the knowledge, skills, and abilities a purchaser must possess.
- ■ Describe the duties and responsibilities of purchasers.
- ■ Describe ethical considerations related to purchasing.
- ■ Identify issues involved in administering purchasing activities.

Test Your Knowledge

1. **True or False:** The purchaser's decisions impact other personnel within the operation. *(See pp. 16–17.)*

2. **True or False:** The purchaser does not need to be concerned with quality standards; this is the concern of the chef and quality assurance manager. *(See p. 20.)*

3. **True or False:** The purchaser must take advantage of any discount offered. *(See pp. 23–24.)*

4. **True or False:** Establishing reciprocity is completely legal. *(See p. 21.)*

5. **True or False:** Cash discounts are a serious ethical transgression. *(See p. 24.)*

Key Terms

Blanket order discount	Job description	Quantity discount
Buyer's authority	Job specification	Reciprocity
Buyer's responsibility	Kickback	Steward sales
Cash discount	Promotional discount	Volume discount
Free sample	Purchasing skill sets	

Introduction

The purchasing function does not happen in isolation in a restaurant or foodservice operation. Whether buying is performed by an owner/manager or organized into a larger buying department, the actions and decisions made related to purchasing impact all of the operation's employees, from managers to hourly staff. Likewise, all the vendors who provide the operation with its goods and services are affected.

The job of purchasing includes many duties that require a variety of skills and abilities. Performing purchasing activities includes administrative work and maintaining supplier relationships, as well as dealing with potential conflicts of interest, among other issues. Therefore, you must possess certain professional qualities and follow firm guidelines and ethical standards to effectively purchase goods and services for your operation.

In this chapter, you will explore the internal and external relationships that drive the purchasing function, the duties that make up this function, and the characteristics needed to perform those duties. You will also learn about the reasons and safeguards for maintaining ethical and professional behavior, as well as issues you might encounter while administering purchasing responsibilities.

Purchasing in a Foodservice Operation

Regardless of a restaurant or foodservice operation's size, someone must perform a certain number of purchasing activities. These activities will either directly or indirectly impact all the various facets of an operation. Therefore, it is important for anyone in the purchasing role to establish and maintain relationships with his or her fellow employees in order to better meet the needs of the operation and, ultimately, the needs of the operation's customers.

Exhibit 2a

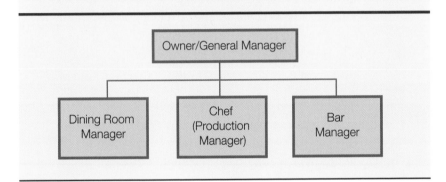

Organizational Chart for Purchasing in Small- to Medium-Sized Independent Operations

Exhibit 2b

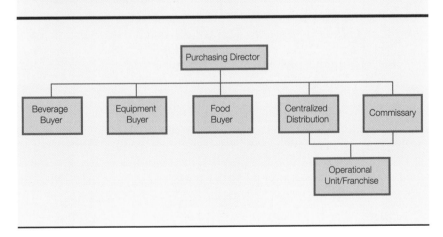

Organizational Chart for Purchasing in a Chain Operation

Organization of the Purchasing Function

In independent or single unit operations, the purchasing agent is often the owner/manager. In some medium-sized independent operations, responsibilities for purchasing are divided among the owner and various unit managers. For instance, the owner might be responsible for purchasing food items, while the bar manager might be responsible for beverage purchasing. A typical purchasing organizational chart for small- to medium-sized independent operations looks like the one in *Exhibit 2a*.

The purchasing function's structure in chain operations might include a purchasing vice president or director, who in some cases performs all purchasing activities, or in other cases directs or monitors them for all units and/or franchisees. An organizational chart for this model might look like the one in *Exhibit 2b*.

How Purchasing Affects an Operation's Employees

Since the purchasing function affects all aspects of the operation, it is, therefore, safe to say that it also affects all of an operation's employees. Part of your responsibilities as a purchaser is to ensure that you provide the right goods and services to the operation's employees in a manner approved by your supervisor. Failure to do this can lead to inefficient work processes, budget difficulties, and employee and customer dissatisfaction.

Specifically, you must consider how your purchasing efforts affect the following groups:

- **The general manager.** Since purchasing has a significant impact on the budget, your general manager, who is typically charged with monitoring an operation's overall budget, will be carefully watching your spending and performance. The GM will also expect any purchaser to be an effective representative of the operation when dealing with vendors and other employees, as well as to circumvent any unethical, legally embarrassing, or unprofessional situation.

- **Other managers.** As a purchaser, you must work cooperatively with your fellow managers, some of whom have no buying authority, to ensure the success of the operation. For example, a chef or production manager who purchases fruit and other garnishes for the entire operation must verify with the bar manager what that area needs. Likewise, the bar manager might purchase the wines and spirits used in the kitchen, items which the chef will have to specify.

- **Hourly employees.** As a purchaser and a member of management, you must ensure that employees have the tools and products needed to do their jobs, which includes everything from lockers to whisks to order pads.

- **Other departments or teams.** As a purchaser, you are in a somewhat unique position in that you must work with most, if not all, departments within an operation. This poses a number of challenges and opportunities. Each department has a limited view of the operation and sees it from its own perspective, whereas you must have an overall or "big picture" view of the operation. Although these relationships possess the potential for friction, they also offer an opportunity for better understanding of the needs and goals of an operation and its divisions. Occasionally, for example, you might need to work with the marketing, sales, or creative teams if and when an alteration to the menu is required, appropriately revising which products and services to order based on the menu change. These kinds of revisions then lead you to work with the kitchen team to ensure that the correct products are being ordered.

Activity

It's Not My Fault

It is not uncommon for conflicts to arise between the purchaser and the production managers who use the products and services purchased.

In this role-play activity, a conflict has emerged between the purchaser and the chef because of a disproportionate amount of food spoilage and waste, which has resulted in food cost increases that are subtracting from the operation's profit. Individuals who assume the roles should take a few minutes to write a brief script based on the role descriptions.

1 A discussion ensues between the purchasing manager and chef, who vehemently debate their respective positions.

2 The owner/manager learns of the conflict and intervenes.

Roles: Purchaser, Chef, and Owner/Manager

Purchaser role description: You are a conscientious and budget-oriented, full-time purchaser who makes a point of obtaining good buys. You believe that the chef is responsible for the food cost increases. You maintain that the chef does not control the kitchen staff during food production, which causes unnecessary spoilage and waste and results in increased food costs.

Chef role description: You are an outstanding chef who argues that the purchaser buys inferior products.

Owner/Manager role description: You are a reasonable and impartial owner/manager who needs to determine what and who to believe, as well as what to do.

After viewing the role-play, discuss the problem and possible solutions. Use the following questions as a guide:

1 What is the main issue?

2 What can be done in the future to circumvent this potential conflict?

3 Why is it important for the purchaser to maintain relationships with colleagues, as well as with his or her supervisor and hourly employees?

The Purchaser's Qualifications and Job Duties

For each job in a restaurant or foodservice operation, there are tools that describe the job in detail and the characteristics of the individual best suited to perform it. A **job specification** lists the desired knowledge, skills, and abilities a person should possess to successfully perform the functions of a specific job.

The Purchaser's Job Specification

A person performing the purchasing function must possess qualities that categorically can be placed in four **purchasing skill sets**: technical, conceptual, interpersonal, and other qualities. Since the tasks a purchaser must perform typically require proficiency in all these areas, the job specification for a purchaser, regardless of the type of operation, should be comprised of some combination of the four of them.

Technical Skills

Whether you purchase all the goods and services for an operation or you are responsible for a smaller, specific group of items, you must understand what you need to buy. You should also understand the intricacies of each of those products or services and how employees will use those items (see Chapter 1 for various lists of potential items). In addition, you will need to determine calculations such as prices and quantities. Examples of technical skills might include:

- Costing a recipe
- Preparing bid sheets
- Calculating order quantities
- Implementing new technologies to improve purchasing efficiency and inventory management

Conceptual Skills

Conceptual skills relate to the overall operation or "big picture" view of an operation. Ideally, a purchaser understands how his or her job affects the overall success of the operation. Conceptual skills include:

- Budgeting expenditures
- Forecasting sales
- Organizing the purchasing function

Think About It...

What are some additional technical, conceptual, interpersonal, and other skills that a buyer should possess?

Interpersonal Skills

Interpersonal skills are related to how well a purchaser works internally with the employees, as well as externally with established and potential vendors. Interpersonal skills include:

- Training receiving staff
- Dealing with vendors and delivery agents (drivers)
- Cooperating with other managers

Other Qualities

Purchasers must also have other important qualities in order to succeed at their jobs. These traits include:

- Education
- Work experience
- Ethical character (integrity, honesty)
- Desire to work for and advance in the particular operation

Activity

Purchaser Wanted

Based on the skills needed to be a purchaser, create a job ad for the purchasing manager at Elenora's Eclectic Eatery, a large, independent operation that serves an assortment of menu items on a regular basis. It is also known for its flair in creating specialty seasonal recipes.

The Purchaser's Job Description

A **job description** describes the specific duties an employee must perform, typically in the form of objectives and operational guidelines. A purchaser's job description will be shaped by the specific operation's policies and needs and should include, but not be limited to, the types of duties listed in *Exhibit 2c*. Another example of a purchaser's job description from a listing of occupational titles found on the U.S. Department of Labor's Web site is shown in *Exhibit 2d*.

Exhibit 2c

Examples of Purchaser's Job Duties

- Negotiate contracts
- Investigate suppliers' facilities
- Define and monitor cost and inventory controls
- Maintain supplier price lists, files, etc.
- Research and identify new products
- Follow code of ethics

- Coordinate activities involved with procuring services and goods
- Monitor the operating budget
- Develop purchase specifications
- Identify, select, and train purchasing staff personnel
- Forecast trends
- Review requisitions

- Determine method of procurement
- Monitor storeroom inventories
- Establish inventory stock levels
- Follow shipping procedures
- Adhere to quality standards
- Control products

Exhibit 2d

Example of a Purchasing Agent's Job Description

162.157-038 Purchasing Agent; alternate titles: Buyer

Coordinates activities involved with procuring goods and services, such as raw materials, equipment, tools, parts, supplies, and advertising for establishment. Reviews requisitions. Confers with vendors to obtain product or service information, such as price, availability, and delivery schedule. Selects products for purchase by testing, observing, or examining items. Estimates values according to knowledge of market price. Determines method of procurement, such as direct purchase or bid. Prepares purchase orders or bid requests. Reviews bid proposals and negotiates contracts within budgetary limitations and scope of authority. Maintains manual or computerized procurement records, such as items or services purchased, costs, delivery, product quality or performance, and inventories. Discusses defective or unacceptable goods or services with inspection or quality control personnel, users, vendors, and others to determine source of trouble and take corrective action. May approve invoices for payment. May expedite delivery of goods to users.

Source: U.S. Department of Labor

Ethical Considerations Related to Purchasing

The rules and guidelines concerning ethics in purchasing are there to protect all the parties involved. Most operations have a written code of ethics that purchasers must commit to following. These rules will help guide your behavior when you are faced with certain questionable circumstances, as outlined in the following sections.

Exhibit 2e

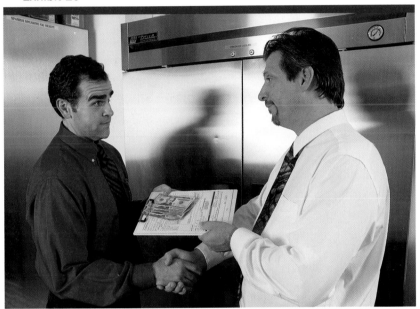

Kickbacks are the most serious ethical transgression.

Kickbacks

Kickbacks are money or other gifts received by an individual in return for purchasing from a specific vendor. Kickbacks are often perceived as the most serious ethical transgression a purchaser can commit. This practice is also illegal. (See *Exhibit 2e.*)

Accepting Gifts

Accepting gifts from vendors should be avoided. Accepting gifts differs from accepting kickbacks in that there is no real expectation that the person receiving the gift will purchase something from the vendor, though the distinction can be hard to see at times. Accepting a gift from a generous vendor with whom you have a relationship may cause you to feel a psychological obligation to that vendor. Therefore, an operation's ethical code should direct you to decline gifts to avoid any appearance of a kickback, as well as to avoid any personal conflicts.

Reciprocity

Reciprocity is an arrangement whereby you agree to buy from a vendor in return for some kind of business from that vendor. For example, the vendor may promise to hold his or her company's holiday party at your restaurant, or the vendor may promise to refer business to the restaurant. Reciprocity generally complicates the client/vendor relationship and should be avoided.

Think About It...

Is it ethical for a purchaser to take advantage of vulnerable suppliers—those that may be in a slump?

Free Samples

Vendors will often offer free samples—small quantities of goods or equipment at no charge—to restaurants. It is best to avoid accepting free samples unless the operation has a genuine interest in considering that product for future purchase.

Personal Purchases

Think About It...

Can allowing personal purchases lead to dishonesty? If so, how?

Some companies allow their employees to take advantage of the company's purchasing power so the employees can buy goods from the operation's vendors for their personal use at discounted prices. This is also known as **steward sales.** These types of purchases are typically limited to designated dates throughout the year, such as holidays. In general, however, this practice should be avoided. Many operations discourage steward sales because some employees might be tempted to make purchases on behalf of their extended family and friends. An exception to this policy, however, would be when the operation chooses to sell goods to its employees in an effort to relieve itself of "dead stock" or overages.

The Administration of Purchasing Activities

While it is important for you to know how to handle the ethical challenges to the purchasing function that occasionally arise, most of your time as a purchaser will be spent dealing with the many day-to-day administrative activities of the job, which can be overwhelming if not managed appropriately. There are also some common problems related to purchasing that you must know how to address quickly in order to ensure the purchasing function runs smoothly in your operation.

Responsibility vs. Authority

When handling the purchasing for your operation—whether you buy for a department or for the whole company—you must understand the extent and/or limitations of your decision-making power. Responsibility and authority are distinctly different, although they are often mistakenly seen as the same thing. **Buyer's responsibility** describes the set of activities that the purchaser manages, whereas **buyer's authority** describes the limits of power the purchaser has to accomplish those activities. For example, you might be responsible for purchasing kitchen equipment, but you will most likely be limited in the amount of money you can spend on a single

Exhibit 2f

Vendors sometimes bypass the buyer and make deals directly with the chef.

purchase without supervisory approval. Understanding and abiding by these boundaries will help you to be successful at purchasing the right products according to the operation's expectations.

Backdoor Selling

A vendor might be tempted to bypass you and deal directly with the individual who will use the product, such as a food supplier who circumvents a buyer in order to deal directly with the chef. (See *Exhibit 2f.*) Most operations seek to avoid backdoor selling because it can negatively affect an operation's bargaining position and the price the operation pays for products. It also might create tension between the purchaser and the person who is making the unauthorized purchase.

Vendor Discounts

Throughout your operation's relationship with a vendor, you might be presented with various types of discounts for the products and services you purchase. The decision to take advantage of a discount (or to let one pass) requires careful consideration of the opportunity's benefits and/or pitfalls. Some types of discounts are:

■ **Quantity discounts.** A supplier may offer a **quantity discount** if an operation purchases a specified, large amount of a particular product. By purchasing a large amount of a product, you are most likely receiving that item at a low per-unit cost. Your storage facilities, however, must be able to handle the unusual amount of the item in a way that does not jeopardize its quality or the quality of other stored products.

■ **Volume discounts.** Like quantity discounts, **volume discounts** are awarded based on the total amount of product purchased. With this kind of discount, you may purchase more than a single product type. The purchase order can include a long list of various items preordered in small amounts. When these items are summed, however, the supplier discounts the total cost. This discount is also known as a **blanket order discount.** To take advantage of a volume discount, an operation might have to commit to ordering a certain amount during a given time period or to some other limitation.

■ **Cash discounts.** A **cash discount** is offered from a vendor for preparing an order, paying cash on delivery (COD), or paying within a specified period of time. The benefit of this discount must be balanced against the operation's cash position and estimated cash needs.

■ **Promotional discounts.** **Promotional discounts** are reductions offered on a specific product or products for a limited period of time. These savings are short-term. The price cut may in some cases be dramatic, but you must consider the long-term cost (of storage, for example) of buying the product.

Activity

What to Do?

An operation's code of ethics guides and safeguards purchasers from perceived acts of impropriety. Given the scenarios below, determine the circumstances under which the purchaser may agree to an arrangement or practice.

1 Marcus Washington is the purchasing manager for The Bethesda Grill. A large vendor has offered Marcus a 5 percent cash discount on invoices paid within ten days of delivery.

_____

_____

_____

2 Darlene Kelly has worked in various foodservice operations most of her life and has always made personal purchases, also known as steward sales, at Thanksgiving, Christmas, and other holidays. She has purchased steaks, roasts, or hams for her own family's celebrations from the operation's suppliers. She recently became employed at a new restaurant.

_____

_____

_____

Vendor Service: Late Deliveries, Substitutions, and Back Orders

Terms of service with a vendor must be established prior to placing an order. Delivery schedules, product continuity, and specifications for appropriate substitutions should be established in a contract at the beginning of the buying relationship. You must then monitor vendor performance to ensure that these established criteria for products and services are being met.

Ways to do this include:

- **Spot-check deliveries to ensure the appropriate product is being delivered.** For example, you might weigh a few steaks from a recently delivered box—choose cuts from the middle of the box, not just those from the top layer—to ensure the proper weight has been shipped.

- **Maintain good communication with the receiving staff.** Be sure to talk with those in charge of receiving products. They are the best source of information about how a vendor is performing— if trucks are on time, if food safety is being maintained during transport, etc.

- **Keep in contact with the vendor.** Take the time to report any issues with shipments to the supplier. By showing your vigilance to the operation's standards, vendors will be more likely to maintain them.

Receiving and Storing Inadequacies

Proper receiving and storing facilities and procedures are necessary to ensure that products are properly inspected, evaluated, and stored. It is vital that you understand the physical characteristics and limitations of your receiving and storing areas so you can order the correct amount of product and have adequate facilities to hold certain products without losing safety or quality. Become familiar with the capabilities of your various storage areas, and be sure the equipment is in good working order.

You must also ensure that your receiving and storeroom personnel have the tools they need to perform their assigned jobs. Various thermometers, dollies, and appropriate shelving are just a few examples of the many kinds of equipment this staff needs. Those with signing authority for deliveries must also have accurate specification information.

Finally, you must monitor employee performance in these areas to ascertain whether proper procedures are being followed. Training is key to proper performance. Maintaining good communication and providing continuous, constructive feedback are also two important ways to accomplish this.

Inefficient Use of Time

Time is a critical factor for purchasers. You will often need to move quickly when presented with an opportunity from a vendor or when a problem occurs with a storage facility. Additionally, you will be expected to complete purchasing tasks despite any issues that arise.

To accomplish all these objectives, practice smart time management. Create task lists that divide your large responsibilities into smaller tasks that can be completed on a daily or weekly level. By dividing large activities into a controllable size, you can organize your work schedule more effectively. Once you have this list, be sure to follow through on it. Evaluate your success against the plan to see which tasks took more or less time than you expected. Many managers also find that time management tools such as a PDA or a time planner help them organize their time more effectively. Finally, be sure to keep meetings on target and on schedule. Meetings with vendors and in-house departments are an integral part of the buying process, but an unfocused, lengthy session can wreak havoc on your daily plans.

Summary

Whether buying is performed by an owner/manager or organized into a larger buying department, the actions and decisions related to purchasing impact all of the operation's employees, from managers to hourly staff. Part of your responsibilities as a purchaser is to ensure that you provide the right goods and services to the operation's employees in a manner approved by your supervisor. Failure to do this can lead to inefficient work processes, budget difficulties, and employee and customer dissatisfaction.

A person performing the purchasing function must possess qualities that categorically can be placed in four purchasing skill sets: technical, conceptual, interpersonal, and other qualities. A purchaser's job description will be shaped by the specific operation's policies and needs and should include duties that relate to these skill sets.

The rules and guidelines concerning ethics in purchasing are there to protect all the parties involved. Most operations have a written code of ethics that purchasers must commit to following. Kickbacks, accepting gifts, reciprocity, free samples, and personal purchases are all areas of ethical concern.

While it is important for you to know how to handle these ethical challenges, most of your time as a purchaser will be spent dealing with the many day-to-day administrative activities of the job, which can be overwhelming if not managed appropriately. There are also some common challenges related to purchasing that you must know how to address quickly in order to ensure the purchasing function runs smoothly in your operation. These range from vendor management to receiving and storing maintenance to effective time management.

Review Your Learning

1 Which of these lists the duties to be performed for a particular position?

A. Job description

B. Job specification

C. Skills listing

D. Job posting

2 When should a purchaser accept free samples?

A. When inventory turnover is low

B. Always

C. When the operation has a genuine interest in using the product

D. When the item has a high value

3 The ability to cost a menu item is considered a(n)

A. conceptual skill.

B. interpersonal skill.

C. technical skill.

D. necessary skill.

4 When a vendor attempts to sell a product directly to the end user rather than to the purchaser, it is called

A. backdoor selling.

B. direct selling.

C. circumventive selling.

D. targeted selling.

5 Paying an invoice on the day it is delivered can result in a

A. quantity discount.

B. blanket order discount.

C. cash discount.

D. flat discount.

6 Which of these might be considered an interpersonal skill?

A. Training a receiving clerk

B. Researching prices

C. Following a budget

D. All of the above

7 Which of these is an issue involved in administering the purchasing function?

A. Backdoor selling

B. Receiving and storing inadequacies

C. Inefficient use of time

D. All of the above

8 Which of these is *not* an ethical transgression?

A. Free samples

B. Reciprocity

C. Volume discounts

D. Accepting gifts

Notes

Quality Standards in Purchasing

3

Inside This Chapter

- Quality Standards
- Factors Affecting Quality Standards
- The Make-or-Buy Decision

After completing this chapter, you should be able to:

- Identify and communicate quality standards.
- Identify factors contributing to the establishment of quality standards.
- State why it is important to convey and adhere to quality standards.
- Describe buyer considerations when conducting a make-or-buy analysis.

Test Your Knowledge

1 **True or False:** The federal government sets standards for all products purchased by foodservice operations. *(See p. 31.)*

2 **True or False:** The most important quality consideration is how a particular item will be used. *(See p. 34.)*

3 **True or False:** Company personnel, consultants, suppliers, or buyers may write quality standards. *(See p. 32-33.)*

4 **True or False:** Buyers have little influence over written quality standards. *(See p. 33.)*

5 **True or False:** If you buy an item versus making it, you need not adhere to quality standards. *(See p. 46.)*

Key Terms

Acceptable trim

Consumer trends

Count

Edible yield

Individually quick frozen (IQF)

Intended use

Make-or-buy analysis

Market form

Packer's brand name

Portion-controlled (PC)

Product specification

Quality standards

Shelf life

Stockout

Throughput

Value-added product

Introduction

As you have seen in previous chapters, purchasers establish the scope of quality in the products used in their operation. Using product specification sheets, prep sheets, adhering to the menu descriptions, or even employing the procedures outlined in your SOP manual are great tools to maintain the product quality your operation seeks to uphold once the products are in house. But what is done to ensure that these products will hold true to your operation's intentions before a purchasing decision is made?

One of the keys to purchasing the right products is quality standards. "Quality," in this sense, is a term used to reflect the value or worth placed on a product or service. The idea of what quality represents varies. In defining what quality means for an operation, the establishment must create a quality standard for every product or service offered. A quality standard is formulated when all the variables involved with satisfying the operation's target market and consumer interests and expectations are researched and developed.

Once determined, quality standards enable you to make effective purchasing decisions for your operation. Establishing solid quality standard specifications enables an operation to maintain control of quality, pricing and overall costs with ease, creating the consistency that customers grow to expect when they purchase their favorite food items. Adhering to set quality standards allows the purchaser to make the effective purchasing decisions that are best for the operation as well as his or her consumers.

Successful operations select the best products for their establishment early on by determining the quality standards for each product purchased and used at the operation. Maintaining consistent, reliable products starts in the purchasing phase of business based upon these standards. This process, while constantly evolving, will be one of the most important processes an operation undergoes to ensure they are offering the right products for the right menu items every time.

Quality Standards

When purchasing products and services needed for your operation, the purchaser must ensure that they are at the proper quality level expected of such an establishment. Often, suppliers offer many products and services in a variety of different quality levels. Therefore, your operation must determine each standard for the quality of products and services it buys. These **quality standards** identify and communicate required product characteristics and specifications to your staff and suppliers. They also support the operation's concept in reflection of the operation's locale, customers, surrounding market, and competition. For example, the product and service needs of an independent casual dining establishment located in a local strip mall will differ significantly from those of an upscale steakhouse located in a luxury hotel. While each operation may have similar menu offerings, the level of food quality, service, and environment for each will differ based upon the defined characteristics of their quality standards.

Because quality standards describe information about items that are necessary to an operation, they must be properly written and recorded. Well-documented quality standards are helpful because they:

- Provide a written record of purchasing criteria so the operation maintains control over the quality and cost incurred with all purchases

- Clearly communicate product and service standards and requirements to your staff and suppliers alike so as to avoid ordering and shipping errors

- Identify your operation's specific product or service requirements for use in a bid

- Allow you to clearly define terms with suppliers to establish a replacement policy for products that do not meet your quality standards

- Improve the ability of employees to identify and prepare menu items

Think About It...

The time and money spent establishing quality standards in the beginning reduces time and money wasted in the end.

Determining Quality Standards

Because quality standards are made up of many important factors, you should first carefully determine them based on your operation's requirements and needs for products and services. Determining and writing accurate quality standards can be a complex process that requires close attention. Establishing standards can help you control your operation's quality and costs, making it more than worth the time taken to create them.

To determine quality standards, a single person or a group within the operation must identify the operation's required level of quality. Using the previous example, the casual dining establishment may determine that lower grade meat is appropriate for its menu, customers, location, and type of business. It might also decide it needs two-ply paper napkins for tabletop dispensers. The upscale steakhouse, however, may determine that only prime grade meat is appropriate for its operation. It also needs thick, white linen napkins for each place setting. Each operation has to determine the level of quality for its necessary products and services and then identify the specifications for that quality.

In an independent operation, an owner or manager typically determines quality standards. In a chain operation, top management and departments on the corporate level such as quality assurance, research and development, and purchasing determine quality standards. Though some chain operations allow for individual locations to employ local vendors for certain necessary products or services, each of these should still fall within the realm of the operation's established quality standards. For example, some chain operations may designate a certain grade steak be used in all Philly Cheese Steak orders. To preserve quality and freshness, the operation may opt to order the same quality steak from a local vendor whose supply meets the standards set for the entire chain.

Exhibit 3a

Assistance in Writing Quality Standards

- American Cutlery Manufacturers Association

- American Institute of Baking

- American Seafood Distributors Association

- Foodservice Equipment Distributors Association

- National Livestock and Meat Board

- National Pasta Association

- National Poultry & Food Distributors Association

- U.S. Department of Agriculture

- U.S. Department of Commerce

- U.S. Food and Drug Administration

- Wine & Spirits Wholesalers of America, Inc.

Others who may help determine and write quality standards include purchasers, suppliers, external consultants, and other company personnel. Purchasers typically make recommendations for quality standards and often bring unique knowledge to the process. They are often knowledgeable about product quality levels, grades, common market forms, availability, relative value of different brands, and as purchased (AP) versus edible portion (EP) costs.

Some quality standards have already been developed and are available in government guidelines and industry publications. *Exhibit 3a* lists several industry organizations with information that can help you get started in determining and writing your quality standards. These resources are available to the public and can be reviewed, reproduced, or used as templates. It is a good idea to review these resources when you determine quality standards to see if any of them apply to your operation. While there is no designated system that will work for every single operation when applying these standards, utilization of all available resources, including the Internet, will help you to create your operation's standards.

Product Specifications

Once you have established your quality standards, you should determine the specifications for those standards. **Product specifications** identify the required characteristics of a particular product or service. Specifications help to clearly support quality standards. As with quality standards, product specifications also help communicate product and service information to your staff and suppliers. Since quality standards only speak to what is necessary for the operation, and not to how an item is purchased, product specifications will.

Product specifications in larger organizations often include exclusive services that a supplier offers as well, such as free delivery, preferred shipping schedules, terms of payment (rebate, invoicing options, other discounts), or offer items that are proprietary to just your operation.

As each concept differs from one restaurant to the next, product specifications also vary for each operation and may depend on the type of establishment. Some specifications may be very detailed and formal and provide precise information about quality standards. This specific information includes an item's yield, packaging, color, quality level, grade, count, size, temperature or processing requirements, shipping or inspection methods, etc. (See *Exhibit 3b* on the next page.) Governments, hospitals, or large chain operations that work with approved suppliers are examples of operations that might use these types of specifications.

Exhibit 3b

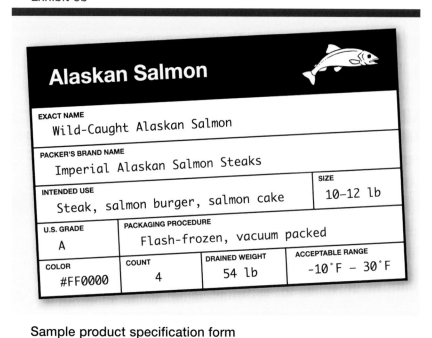

Sample product specification form

Smaller independent operations might use more informal specifications. These establishments might use general specifications that only list a few requirements such as a product's exact name and its intended use. Each operation should determine specifications and document them in the way that is appropriate for its business and satisfies its quality standards.

Remember that as a purchaser, you are also a customer, and you must indicate your exact needs to ensure you receive what you want for your operation. Following are some characteristics to include in product specifications.

The Intended Use of the Product or Service

Understanding what items are necessary for your operation stems from ensuring that the item's intended use is clearly defined. The **intended use** describes how a product or service is meant to be used, developed, or consumed. A product's intended use is its most important characteristic to consider when specifying quality standards. The way you plan to use the product or service drives all decisions for selecting the product and its supplier.

When determining the product specifications, the intended use of the item is the first thing taken into account. Quality standards are set accordingly and then further detailed to create the product specifications for the item. For example, in some cases, operations may find that purchasing **portion-controlled (PC)** items better serves their needs. Portion-controlled items are preportioned and individually wrapped or packaged. Depending on the operation's intended use, offering preportioned items may be more cost-effective than purchasing the item in bulk. For instance, when catering a breakfast event, open jelly dishes can be placed on each table or dish for use with breakfast rolls. If the jelly is not consumed, however, it is thrown out. Offering portion-controlled jelly would allow for the jelly packets to be used again. Once an economy-size jar of jelly is opened, the freshness of the contents within will expire much faster than if the jelly is served in individual packets that will not be opened until consumption. While the quality standard may specify "grape jelly," the product specifications can further detail purchasing needs to accommodate the product's intended use.

The Exact Name for an Item

When applicable, you should use the exact name of the item or service you want to buy. For example, if you are writing a specification for grapes, you may receive the wrong ones if you only write "grapes" in your specification. Instead, you should write the exact grape you need, such as "grapes, Thompson seedless." Using exact names helps to ensure that you receive the correct item, avoids frustration and misinterpretation for you and the supplier, and keeps customers satisfied.

Consider menu item of chicken nuggets. When ordering chicken, you will need to specify what type of chicken is needed. Choices range anywhere from "grilled chicken," "boneless chicken," "fillets," or even "chicken wings." Because boneless, battered nuggets are offered to the customer, the purchaser may specify "battered chicken nuggets" as the exact name for the type of chicken needed. Specifying what you want by providing the exact name of the product will further narrow possibilities for error.

The Brand of the Item

While providing the exact name of the item in product specifications is important, brand-name specification should be documented where applicable. People often buy products or services by their brand names since these names can indicate levels of quality.

Many producers or suppliers also offer items featuring their own brand name on products and services. The **packer's brand name** is the supplier's own label product and is available in levels that reflect the supplier's own quality categories. These categories generally vary from good quality to the best quality. You may find that quality standards include a packer's brand name product. Make sure to indicate the correct packer's brand name and the appropriate quality level when writing the specification.

While packer's brand products may satisfy many of the needs of your operation, it is important to consider whether the packer's brand name will be presented to customers in any way, like with table settings: salt packages, creamers, butter, or ketchup labels. In this case, it might be more appealing to the customer to provide name brands that they are familiar with and equate with high quality.

Sometimes the brand of the product or service you specify is not available. There may be other brands, including packer's brand names that meet the quality standards of the brand, product, or service you specified. If you decide that another brand can be used as a substitute, your specifications should clearly state that a product could be substituted with an equivalent or specific product or brand if your choice is not available. More information about the process of specifying acceptable substitutes will be discussed later in this chapter.

Packaging

Packaging choices are just as plentiful as the products you choose. Specific products can be packaged differently based on the science of preparing products for storage, transportation, and eventual use/sale. Considerations are typically centered on the item type, weight, preservation needs, intended use, and the amount or portion of the item within the overall package.

As always, the intended use of a product is first taken into consideration when choosing a product's packaging type. For instance, a quick-serve carryout establishment will likely need boxes of individual ketchup packets. A casual eat-in diner may need small ketchup bottles to put on the tables for customer use. If items are intended to remain in their original container, packaging will need to accommodate that intention. Using the example above, ketchup can be packaged in economy-size cans or jars, individual bottles, or individual packets within a box. (See *Exhibit 3c.*) The packaging needed for each container in which the product is stored will be respectively different.

In many cases, packaging is standardized based upon the product type or fragility. Packaging for items such as eggs, dairy products, or highly perishable items must satisfy certain requirements that will protect them from loss of look/form, contamination, damage from subpar temperatures, moisture, and possible crushing while being handled, stored, or transported. When shipping frozen meats, packaging considerations must address what packaging can withstand storing and transporting very cold items without losing its integrity. Loss of quality (and possibly safety) occurs when these things are not taken into consideration. Carefully packaged products maintain their culinary-quality characteristics and their appearance and have a comparatively longer **shelf life,** or amount of time during which the product can remain suitable for use.

Exhibit 3c

A product's container often influences its packaging needs for shipment.

Size of the Product

Specifications may also need to include the required size of an item or package. For example, your quality standards and intended use for the product determine that you need twelve-ounce strip steaks and crushed tomatoes for your operation. The precise size measurement must be specified in detail using the proper terms applicable for the item type. Size measurements are indicated in terms of weight, volume, or count. While the quality standard may just say "crushed tomatoes," the product specification may say, "six to a case, #10 can." The purchaser must then determine if that amount is necessary and in what way it should be purchased and shipped.

Exact weight measurements, or weight ranges, are necessary when portioning certain items. Products like flour or rice can be provided exactly measured. For example, you know that it takes 2.5 pounds of flour to yield a full batch of bread boules to satisfy the amount of pizza pies needed during your operation's lunch rush and, therefore, can order a number of five-pound bags of flour for your operation. Products such as a side of beef or a whole turkey, on the other hand, may be ordered using an acceptable weight range for your operation.

Some items are sized by their count. A **count** is a measurement of the number of items/units within a certain portion or size. Items such as potato chips, individual bottles of drinking water, or cans of soda are examples of items that are ordered based upon count.

Acceptable Trim

Specifications include the amount of acceptable trim for a product. The **acceptable trim** measures the maximum amount of tolerable waste acceptable in a product upon receipt. Some purchasers may refer to this by mentioning the minimum amount of **edible yield** accepted. This specification is often used for fresh products like carrots or lettuce that may experience varying degrees of rotting along the outside layer(s) depending on how suppliers process them. Some carrots can be ordered in slices, spears, or shredded as a ready-to-serve product, whereas the carrot in its natural state has an edible yield of much less than 100 percent.

Products with little or no waste are more expensive than those with higher waste or lower edible yield. For instance, pineapples have an edible region limited to what is inside its protective skin. While the edible yield is likely to be determined by the size of the pineapple, higher prices are placed on pineapples that are cored (and skinned), which can increase the edible yield by more than if it were provided in its original form. (See *Exhibit 3d.*) Furthermore, orders made based upon weight will promise more useable product when the wasted portions of the product have already been removed.

Exhibit 3d

Low edible yield/
Low price

High edible yield/
High price

Think About It...

Items that require egg breaking during their production process, as well as all poultry and meat items, have federal government grades.

The U.S. Grade of the Item

The U.S. government provides quality measurements or indicators known as USDA (United States Department of Agriculture) grades. There are over three hundred different food and agricultural items, including beef, poultry, eggs and other food items, that are USDA graded. The grades identify various degrees of quality for each item. In general, for items to receive a USDA grade, they must go through inspection by the federal government. Since grades identify degrees of quality, they are also helpful in determining the value of a product. A higher-grade product is more valuable and will likely cost more than a lower-grade product. (See *Exhibit 3e.*)

The law generally does *not* require government grades for purchasing, and the USDA's program is voluntary in nature. For this reason, you should have other quality measures in place in addition to the USDA grade, when applicable. To some degree, the grade alone might not be enough to meet your quality standards.

If ever you wanted to purchase a nongraded item that has the same quality as a given USDA grade, the specification can indicate the USDA grade you want followed by the words "or equivalent," but these determinations are usually made by the seller."

Exhibit 3e

U.S. Grades of Beef

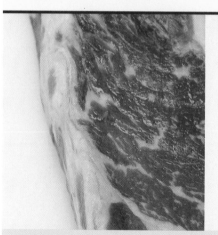 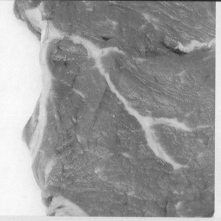 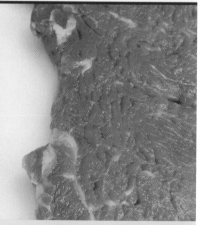

USDA Prime

Prime grade beef is the ultimate in tenderness, juiciness, and flavor. It has a lot of marbling— flecks of fat within the lean— which enhances both flavor and juiciness.

USDA Choice

Choice grade beef has less marbling than Prime but is of very high quality. Choice roasts and steaks from the loin and rib will be very tender, juicy, and flavorful.

USDA Select

Select grade beef is very uniform in quality and somewhat leaner than higher grades. It is fairly tender, but, because it has less marbling, it may lack some of the juiciness and flavor of the higher grades.

Market Form: Type of Preservation or Processing Method

Specifications should describe an item's market form to obtain the intended taste or culinary characteristics of a finished product. The **market form** indicates how an item is processed prior to being packaged. For example, given the carrot example, the purchaser will need to specify if he or she wants shredded, sliced, canned (in water or oil), or frozen carrots. Some other types of market forms include fresh or dried.

Preservation needs can also be met by special processing procedures designed to increase quality maintenance when routing highly perishable food from the manufacturer to the operation. Purchasers may consider vacuum packaging or **Individually Quick Frozen (IQF)** products. IQF is a process, mostly used with fish or fruit, where food is blast-frozen in individual pieces before packaging. By using this method of preservation, operations are able to better maintain the taste, texture, and nutrient values of the food item.

Keeping in mind the market form of an item can have a definite effect on your operation's purchasing decisions. For example, the chef may want to have several trays of Black Tiger Shrimp Cocktail set out on an appetizer table for a catering event of two hundred guests. It is a reasonable assumption that approximately eight hundred shrimp would need to be prepared to accommodate that number of guests. This would require that each shrimp is peeled, deveined, and cooked, which would be a cumbersome and time-consuming task if the shrimp were fresh. The quality standard for the shrimp cocktail appetizer may be "black tiger shrimp, chilled; arranged and served on top of a bed of greens with a crystal bowl of cocktail sauce in the middle and lemon wedges surrounding the edges." The product specification for the shrimp would include, "fully cooked, ready-to-serve black tiger shrimp, peeled and deveined with tail on, and individually quick frozen." The purchaser will order the black tiger shrimp IQF so that when the shrimp arrives all that needs to be done is thawing. As a result, the operation will save time and money in labor choosing this option. (See *Exhibit 3f.*)

Color

If available in different colors, buyers must specify the color they desire for an item. For example, a purchaser has the option to choose between green beans and yellow beans, white grapes and red grapes, or white-shelled eggs and brown-shelled eggs. In cases like the strawberry example, operations may choose to use certain colors in food to create a look that is appealing to the customer in the final product or the display of the entire dish.

Exhibit 3f

IQF products maintain quality while saving preparation time.

Aside from the look of the product, certain products may hold flavor attributes that are notably different in one color than in another. For instance, white grapes are distinctly sweeter in flavor than red grapes. Therefore, menu items prepared with grapes will require specific identification of the color grape needed based upon which flavor attribute provides the intended flavor.

Place of Origin

A purchaser must indicate the place of origin from where a desired item is required on the specification. Examples include Florida oranges, California walnuts, New Zealand lamb, or Maine lobster. (See *Exhibit 3g*.)

There are several reasons why specifying this standard is important:

- The texture and flavor of certain products is specific to its region of origin.

- An operation's policies might dictate that, (for political reasons, for example) its products do not come from a certain place of origin.

- The operation's menu may state that the item comes from a particular place of origin.

- Purchasers may indicate that they desire their products from a nearby location to further guarantee an item's quality and freshness.

Exhibit 3g

Pears grown in regions such as California carry the region's reputation of high-quality fruit.

Acceptable Substitutes

Some purchasers have found it useful to provide the supplier with acceptable substitutes to the original products requested. Providing alternatives for the original requests early on can save a lot of time and effort by alleviating time spent by the supplier contacting the purchaser to secure an acceptable substitute if the normal item is unavailable. Purchasers, however, must be attentive to recipes and menu item listings, as they cannot substitute an item that does not match these. An added expense of this method is the time necessary to test substitutes to ensure they are compatible with quality standards, production, and service needs.

In choosing the best method of securing accurate supply levels, managers typically devise an inventory management system to determine the amount of beverages, food, and nonfood supplies necessary for day-to-day operations. When purchasing goods, it can be to the operation's benefit to have an acceptable substitute in mind to avoid stockouts. A **stockout** occurs when an item has been depleted from inventory.

While stockouts are never a good thing, hastily substituting an item as a quick fix for a stockout does not necessarily serve as a remedy to your operation's issue with inventory shortages. Furthermore, chancing a substitute for an item used when preparing an operation's signature dish may hurt the operation's image of quality in the eyes of new and frequent customers. If you choose to provide an acceptable substitute, a simple rule of thumb that will help with this decision, as with any purchase, is to always make certain that the item still falls well within the guidelines stated in your operation's quality standards.

Unit Pricing

Purchasers may specify that the product be purchased in unit types and priced accordingly on the product specifications. For example, they may denote that the item be purchased per dozen, per case, or per any other pertinent unit based on that item's need and cost. Realistically, it is not the purchaser's decision as to whether or not five hundred portion-controlled packs (PCs) of jelly come in a box at one unit price. The supplier may decide that these are provided in cases of 150. It is then up to purchasers to decide whether they would prefer to purchase four cases of 150 PCs of jelly for a total of 600 PCs, or if they would prefer to purchase an economy-size jar to fulfill this need.

Price Limits

Purchasers may specify the maximum amount they will pay for a given product. If the product exceeds the maximum price the purchaser specifies as allowable, the vendor may not ship the product. If the cost of the product or service comes near the specified price limits, a purchaser might specify that a substitute be issued or might reevaluate whether to stop ordering this product.

Temperature Control Procedures

Purchasers may specify the method of handling for a product by requesting certain temperature controls. A purchaser might, for instance, insist that all dairy products be delivered at or below 41°F (5°C) to preserve freshness and retain quality. This is done because perishable products usually deteriorate and become unsafe quickly outside of certain temperature levels, and food preparation of menu items may be affected.

Specific instructions that relate to food safety and quality are paramount. Meat, poultry, fish, produce, some beverages and other perishable food categories require specific temperature controls. Temperature control procedures are critical in foodhandling. If food is ordered frozen, it must arrive frozen in a refrigerated truck. Once delivered, it is important for the operation to see that these products are quickly stored away to avoid a negative impact on safety and freshness.

Adherence to Quality Standards

Having and adhering to quality specifications can be advantageous to the purchaser and the operation. Every quality standard indicated on the product specification must be adhered to in order to guarantee that the desired product or service quality remains consistent.

Detailing quality standards requires that the purchaser be very familiar with every characteristic of all products, from establishing the AP and EP price to ensuring that the desired quality of a product is available. Specification writing requires adherence to limitations, training needs, and potential problems and costs associated with each product. If it is the operation's decision to write quality specifications, it is the purchaser's responsibility to keep them up to date and ensure that the staff and suppliers know and adhere to them. Failure to reinforce the adherence to an operation's quality standards is as damaging as having no standards at all.

Factors Affecting Quality Standards

A number of factors influence quality standards for foodservice operations. Decision-makers will take these factors into consideration when writing product specifications.

The Item's Intended Use

As with determining product specifications, being wary of the product's intended use and how it will be prepared and served is the most influential factor in determining quality standards. Fruit used for accenting or garnishing plates will require a slightly different quality than that used to make dessert sauces. Fruit used for garnishing will be chosen based upon its appearance, whereas fresh fruit destined to be used as a sauce may be overripe or even damaged.

The Operation's Concept and Goals

The overall concept and goals of the operation guides all decisions. If an operation aims to serve as a fast-casual dining concept, serving premium items but in a fraction of the time it takes at an upscale dining restaurant, considerations must be made as to what products will serve this purpose most effectively. Such an operation is promising speed, convenience, reasonable prices, and premium menu items to its target consumer. The products purchased at such an operation must lend themselves to this concept. For instance, an impinger oven—a conveyer-belt style oven used to toast bread products—may be necessary to provide faster throughput for an establishment that serves sandwiches, bagels, or small pizzas. **Throughput** measures the speed in which service requests are processed. Such a device may alleviate the need for an ongoing baker, cutting labor costs, and thus allowing for the operation to provide a generous price to its customers. The purchaser must consider such factors before writing or offering input regarding quality standards.

The Menu

The operation's menu dictates the items of interest to the purchaser. If the menu specifies "whole Cornish hens," the purchaser is obliged to include specifications to the supplier for "whole Cornish hens." If a name brand is mentioned, such as "Ice Cookie Chocolate Smoothie," the purchaser will be limited to providing only Ice Cookies for this item and must specify that in the quality standards.

Exhibit 3h

Complex menu items require highly skilled employees.

The Employee Skill Level

When making a purchasing decision, purchasers must take into account the skill level of the employees staffed at the operation. In an operation offering products that require extensive preparation, higher-skilled employees are generally required. (See *Exhibit 3h.*) Of course, higher skill levels equal higher wages. Where skill levels are lower, easy-to-use or easy-to-prepare convenience products are used. Although unskilled employees will be paid less than highly skilled employees, these types of food generally cost more. This trade-off issue is often addressed in a make-or-buy analysis, which will be discussed on pp. 46–48.

Budgetary Constraints

Operations in highly competitive markets may need to include cost limits in their product specifications in order to maintain their competitive position, since their menu item prices may be fixed by their competitors. Operations may also want to avoid purchasing products whose prices fluctuate wildly and may specify products within acceptable limits. Fluctuations in any item's price may negatively impact the business' profit.

Customers' Wants and Needs

If ever there was a way to decide what to offer your customers, nothing tops seeking the answers from the customers themselves. Analyze and track consumer trends by providing surveys and customer feedback forms. Find out what your target market is seeking and why they choose to frequent (or not to frequent) your establishment.

Smart operations respond to their customers' wants and needs by providing goods and services that meet those needs and provide for a desired profit. In many cases, these wants and needs are generally influenced by industry and consumer trends. **Consumer trends** define the general direction in which a market or consumer type is headed. It can describe anything from a consumer's behaviors and beliefs to his or her style and attitude. Quality specifications may need to be updated periodically to reflect any changes in preference or style according to these trends.

Larger operations may utilize resources that will help gather specific information about their average customer and his or her trends. Through this, an operation can make better, more relevant choices when purchasing goods to offer its customers. For instance, an operation may find that they are located in an area in which the average household consists of twenty-three- to forty-year-olds with children. Accordingly, the establishment may choose to provide pancakes shaped like a mouse's head or animal-shaped chicken nuggets to provide for a more family-centered consumer. The purchaser may add mouse-shaped cookie cutters to the purchasing list to accommodate this specification. More thorough studies that include the average income level, level of education, or spending habits can also come in handy when deciding the quality of products expected for this type of consumer.

Other popular niches may catch on and cause operations to consider changes in what the customer wants. Recently, when the media announced the statistics relating to obesity in Americans, words like "low-carb" were popping up on menus next to breadless sandwiches. Some operations responded to this immediate concern by changing or enhancing their menu offerings with products that would allow for them to update their nutritional data to appeal to this niche.

Activity

Building Specs for Build-a-Burger

You are the purchaser for Build-a-Burger, an independently owned quick-service carryout establishment, where the motto is "You create 'em—we fry 'em!" You need to update the product specifications for ketchup, cheese, tomatoes, and hamburger meat. Considering all of the influences and factors affecting quality standards that may be included on a product specification, list the quality standards that you would include on a product specification for each of the above items. Be thorough and creative, and be prepared to explain your answers to the owner/manager, who has charged you with writing the operation's quality specifications.

1 Ketchup

_____

_____

_____

2 Cheese

_____

_____

_____

3 Tomatoes

_____

_____

_____

4 Hamburger

_____

_____

_____

Seasonal Availability

The seasonal nature of produce and other items affects fluctuations in price and availability. The need for certain products (especially produce) may more than double during certain months. Decision-makers will need to determine if the season will affect a change in product specification. In such a case, operations may also have more than one menu that is swapped periodically to reflect the seasonal availability of some products.

Availability of Storage

An operation's storage capacity limits the amount of product kept in house. If an operation has limited freezer space, a limited amount of food can be maintained at the required temperature levels necessary to ensure freshness. Preferences may be set to order fresh, ready-to-use products if additional freezer storage is not obtained. On the other hand, if plenty of shelf space is available, some items, such as mushrooms, may be ordered in a can instead of frozen.

The Make-or-Buy Decision

One of the most critical research development projects that a purchaser can undertake is the process of developing a make-or-buy analysis. A **make-or-buy analysis** is an assessment that reveals whether a product should be prepared from scratch or purchased as a partially or fully processed item. In many ways, determining what should be created internally versus what should be bought ready-made may seem to be a simple task, but due to the many variables involved in food management in operations, foregoing careful planning in this step can take a toll on your operation.

A purchaser conducts a make-or-buy analysis to discover the proper balance in food production, yielding the best possible outcome to satisfy the quality standards set for the operation. Preportioned and processed food items are considered **value-added products.** The relationship between edible portion (EP) cost and desired quality is broken into a number of factors when weighing the advantages and disadvantages in purchasing value-added products. In many cases, the costs incurred for paying the higher premium attached to value-added products is offset by other overhead involved in running an operation.

The Case for Buying Food

While it is clear that the decision must be made as to whether an operation intends on making or buying products, the decision as to which method is best is not always so clear. It is important that the operation establishes its desired quality level before deciding whether to make food from scratch. This is generally based on the operation's concept, menu, locality, setting, customer base, budgetary and facility constraints, and worker skill level.

Ultimately, the buyer conducting the analysis needs to take into consideration all the factors and influences that affect quality standards. Many may find that their quality standards are easily met when purchasing value-added products. Some of the advantages incurred by purchasing value-added products are:

- **Consistency.** Value-added products are packaged the same way every time. Therefore, there is a consistent level of quality in each package as well as an even portion of product every time.

- **Cost effectiveness.** Because value-added products are delivered partially or completely processed already and at a consistent preportioned amount, operations can better plan their pars for each day or shift, lessening the amount of waste or leftovers remaining from day to day. Packaged portions generally have an increased level of edible yield, therefore providing for a more reliable quantity of usable product every time. An added bonus is that there is no need to afford the cost of highly skilled employees to prepare these items.

- **Time effectiveness.** As you know, time is money. So redirecting efforts where they are best needed is always beneficial to any operation. Value-added products not only save time needed to prepare from scratch, but also free up time needed to supervise employees to ensure proper handling and consistency. Instead, supervisors and managers are able to be more productive in the operation by increasing sales volume, or improving customer relations by having more of a front-of-the-house presence during operating times.

- **Space savings.** The ability to prepare menu items with little equipment, supervision, or storage space needed to house leftovers means possible space savings in the prep/kitchen area. Such space reduction can allow for more space for other valuable add-ons to your operation, such as a beverage cooler, dessert bar, or increased space for dine-in patrons.

The Case for Making Food from Scratch

While the term value-added can easily be associated with the term "cost-added" when selecting the best method to use in a purchasing decision, you must determine that the product is indeed adding more value than cost. When taking into account the advantages found in purchasing value-added products, you may find that it is a better business decision to go for the value-added, or processed, food. However, making a product internally may prove to be a better choice if the equipment space and skill requirement is minimal and will prove to produce a product that better suits the quality standards. Additionally, it may be more important to the operation to serve some products fresh, as their quality standards require. For instance, being prepared to make portions needed for the fluctuating level of business due to the high number of tourists in your area may hold priority over the cost savings found in buying preprocessed food in quantitative bundles. So in this case, making the product in house may be a better choice.

Owners or chefs may take pride in the fact that they offer noteworthy products and will opt to make their own products from scratch every time, especially their signature dishes, in order to guarantee an exclusive taste to the customer. They may be known for their tangy BBQ sauce or their spicy buffalo wings. Restaurants noted for authenticity may also prefer to make their products in-house. These operations are often more concerned with being the best in town rather than cutting budget costs.

Think About It...

The USDA Acceptance Service allows restaurants and foodservice operations to hire USDA inspectors to assist in writing specifications. Resources are available at *http://www.usda.gov/gac*.

Exhibit 3i

Items can be made from raw ingredients or can be purchased in processed form.

Choosing to make food offers certain advantages over purchasing it. Generally, the food's cost will be lower, the nutritional value of it will be higher, and there will be fewer additives in the food. Arguably, while the quality may not necessarily be better, the taste of the food item might be preferable and, therefore, perceived as higher in quality by the consumer. (See *Exhibit 3i.*)

There is no set science as to whether an operation should make or buy products. Careful planning and thorough research will be beneficial to you and your operation every time. Creating a thorough make-or-buy analysis will help you find the best way to satisfy your operation's quality standards as well as to support the operation's bottom line.

Summary

Quality standards describe the measures of excellence a foodservice operation seeks to satisfy. They not only reflect an operation's locale and clientele, but they also serve as cost controls and tools that can be used to uphold alignment between purchasers and suppliers. Quality standards pronounce quality expectations to customers. They serve as parameters for suppliers that submit bid proposals and list every important consideration of the operation's food and nonfood products and services.

Many factors and influences affect quality standards and must be considered prior to writing the operation's product specifications. To assist them, purchasers may choose to perform a make-or-buy analysis to determine the best possible relationship between a product's desired quality and edible portion cost.

Many people may offer input into what an operation's quality standards should be. However, it is the responsibility of the owner and/or purchaser to ensure that all internal and external stakeholders know and adhere to them.

Review Your Learning

1 What must be included in a quality specification?

  A. Quantity needed

  B. Product weight

  C. Product name

  D. Date needed

2 Which is the most influential factor influencing quality specification?

  A. Product cost

  B. Product place of origin

  C. Employee skill level

  D. Product intended use

3 Which of these is generally true of value-added or convenience products?

  A. Convenience products are harder to track.

  B. Convenience products require less employee skill to prepare.

  C. Convenience products require more employee skill to prepare.

  D. Convenience products are more nutritious.

4 Which is an advantage of having quality specifications?

  A. More consistent product quality

  B. Better communication

  C. Lower costs

  D. All of the above

5 If your menu specifies "Alaskan Crab," then the crab

  A. must be from Alaskan waters.

  B. may be from the Atlantic Ocean.

  C. must be equivalent to Alaskan crab.

  D. may be from the Great Lakes.

6 Which is true of U.S. Grades?

  A. U.S. Grades apply to all food items.

  B. All food that can be graded must be graded.

  C. If available, U.S. Grades should be specified.

  D. U.S. Grades are not a reliable quality measure.

7 The move towards healthier, lower-calorie food is an example of a(n)

  A. fad.

  B. local anomaly.

  C. market swing.

  D. industry or business trend.

8 A make-or-buy analysis

  A. is necessary for all meat products.

  B. compares product costs for making or buying an item.

  C. illustrates industry trends.

  D. enables better communication between the buyer and seller.

9 When conducting a make-or-buy analysis, you must consider which factor(s)?

  A. Staff skill level and labor cost

  B. Facility requirements to make the item

  C. Desired quality level of product

  D. All of the above

10 Why is it important to adhere to quality standards?

_____

_____

_____

_____

Notes

The Procurement Process and Supplier Selection

4

Inside This Chapter

- The Procurement Process
- Supplier Selection

After completing this chapter, you should be able to:

- Outline the process for procuring products and services.
- Differentiate between perishable and nonperishable food products.
- Understand the importance of assessing and documenting purchasing requirements.
- Define perpetual inventory and physical inventory.
- Identify optimal sources of suppliers.

Test Your Knowledge

1 **True or False:** The requirements of the procurement process are met once products and services have been ordered. *(See p. 53.)*

2 **True or False:** You can either select a supplier before or after writing product specifications, depending on the operation's buying plan. *(See p. 57.)*

3 **True or False:** When taking receipt of products, the receiving clerk's job is completed after he or she reads or examines the outside label of the cartons or containers. *(See p. 58.)*

4 **True or False:** The most important consideration in determining the optimal supplier source is to choose the supplier whose bid reflects the lowest AP prices. *(See p. 64.)*

5 **True or False:** The purchasing process for nonperishable food is more routine than it is for perishable food. *(See p. 54.)*

Key Terms

Approved supplier list

Beverage alcohols

Bid buying plan

Capital expenditures

Cost-plus purchasing

Distributor sales
representative (DSR)

Furniture, fixtures, and
equipment (FF&E)

Goods and services needs
assessment

In-process inventory

Nonperishable products

One-stop shop buying plan

Par

Perishable products

Perpetual inventory

Physical inventory

Pilferage

Plan of action (POA)

Procurement process

Purchase order

Purchase requisition

Ready-to-go

Receiving

Request-for-bid

Request-for-price (RFP)

Route salespeople

Shelf life

Spoilage

Stockless purchasing

Storage area regulations

Value-added products

Introduction

Purchasing perishable and nonperishable food products, nonfood products, and services requires a great deal of knowledge and skill. Purchasing these items involves a **plan of action** (POA) that takes into consideration the products that best meet the operation's wants and needs, and the suppliers that can best provide them according to the operation's documented quality standards and buying practices.

The process for procuring products and services requires that internal staff—unit managers, purchasing managers or buyers, inventory and receiving clerks, and chefs or production managers—be trained to assess the operation's goods and services' requirements, as well as the specific procedures for the following important steps related to procurement:

- Assessing

- Selecting

- Ordering

- Receiving

- Storing

- Issuing

The Procurement Process

When executing purchasing duties, the most basic—but most critical—consideration is regularly assessing the operation's needs and purchasing the ideal quality and quantity of product or service from the ideal supplier, for the ideal EP cost, at the ideal time. However, your job is not done, in most cases, until all the products have been satisfactorily and appropriately received, stored, and issued to the internal staff who will use them.

The best procurement process or perfectly written product specifications are ineffective unless the individuals using them are trained. Before purchasing any product or service, all appropriate employees should be trained on and understand the aspects of the operation's procurement process. The **procurement process** outlines the operation's product selection; the ordering, receiving, and storing process; and the issuing of policies and procedures. This process is based on the operation's quality standards, which reflect its mission and goals.

Step 1: Assess the Operation's Needs and Wants

A common first step in the procurement process is determining the operation's needs and wants. To determine the operation's purchasing requirements, a **goods and services needs assessment**, must be completed. This is a review of what the operation has versus what it ideally needs, and is a regularly scheduled step. (See *Exhibit 4a*.) Who conducts this evaluation is based on the size of the operation. Whoever is responsible for this purchasing function must

Exhibit 4a

A goods and services needs assessment must be completed to determine the operation's purchasing requirements.

approach the assessment of the organization's needs from a collaborative perspective. The purchaser must talk and work directly with managers who directly use the purchased items to decide on both immediate and future needs. *Exhibit 4b* provides you with some sample questions that you might ask managers in assessing the needs for their area. It is important to establish a good working relationship with these people because they are your customers. You should establish the appropriate frequency to fulfill their inventory needs.

Once you have completed a thorough assessment of the operation's needs, it is imperative that you go back to those same managers and together write product specifications for all the products identified during the assessment. You need to write specifications for all perishable and nonperishable food products, nonfood products, and furniture, fixtures, and equipment (FF&E). Also known as **capital expenditures, furniture, fixtures, and equipment (FF&E)** are long-life items that often depreciate over a period of time.

Perishable and Nonperishable Products

Perishable products are food products sold or distributed in a form that will perish or decay within a limited period of time as a result of the action of bacteria, light, and air. Perishable products include meat, fish, poultry, dairy, eggs, produce, and beverage alcohols.

Nonperishable products are items that do not support the growth of bacteria. They consist of processed and canned or bottled products and dried goods, which are also known as **value-added products.**

The process for obtaining nonperishable food and FF&E is more habitual and regular than it is for perishable food because AP costs and quality are more stable for these types of items. Therefore, this process is generally more routine and uncomplicated. Most purchasers find that after the initial product specification has been determined for these kinds of items, modification is only necessary when a product must be updated or the quality of the product no longer meets the operation's needs. FF&E items are expensive items that take much research and planning before purchase. These items will be used in the operation for several years. Therefore, styles, trends, and anticipated growth need to be factored into these decisions.

Exhibit 4b

Sample Questions for a Purchaser to Ask in the Assessment Process

Chef	Kitchen Manager	Dining Room Manager	Restaurant Manager	Bar Manager
What products do you need to support the current menu?	What equipment do we need in the kitchen to support preparing, cooking, serving, storing, cooling, and reheating food?	What items do you need for the dining room (i.e., linens, china, glassware, utensils, etc.)?	What major purchases do we need to make immediately? Within the year?	What products do we offer on our drink menu? ■ Distilled spirits ■ Beer (keg vs. bottle) ■ Wine
What levels of inventory do we need to keep on hand at all times to support our menu?	What utensils do we need?	Do we have any tables or furniture that need replacing?	What are the plans for the establishment for the next year?	What are our par levels for each product?
What specials will you be running in the next quarter? What products will be needed to support these specials?	Do we have any equipment that is beyond repair and needs to be replaced?	Do we have enough uniforms for our staff? Do we need new uniforms?		What is the frequency for placing orders for each product?
What are the product specifications that need to be met for all products?	Are there any equipment or tools that can make the jobs of the kitchen staff more efficient?	Do we need anything new in the dining room to add to our décor? Do we need to change our décor?		What other bar supplies do we need? ■ Mixers/mixes ■ Condiments ■ Glassware ■ Bar equipment
When will the next menu change occur?	What products do we need for sanitation purposes?	What accommodations do we need for special events?		
How frequently should we order products (i.e., daily, weekly, monthly, product specific, etc.)?	What uniforms do we need to purchase for your team?	What uniforms do we need to purchase for your team?		What bar uniforms do we need? ■ Aprons ■ Shirts ■ Ties

Step 2: Select Criteria/Quality Standards

Purchasers have a great deal to say regarding the quality standards for an operation's products. They ensure the operation's overall quality by selecting and purchasing items that meet those standards.

When purchasing perishable and nonperishable food products, nonfood items, or FF&E, purchasers consider one or more selection factors. (See *Exhibit 4c.*) Senior management will ultimately, however, decide which selection factors are critical to its success.

Exhibit 4c

Selection Factors

■ Intended use	■ Supplier services	■ Versatility
■ Exact name	■ Minimum weight per case	■ Compactness
■ Packer's brand name (or equivalent)	■ Product yield	■ Compatibility
■ U.S. Government Grades (or equivalent)	■ Overrun	■ Appearance
	■ Chemical additives	■ Portability
■ Product size	■ AP price	■ Ease of cleaning
■ Size of container	■ One-stop shopping	■ Ease of maintenance
■ Type of container	■ Supplier services	■ Degree of automation
■ Type of packaging material	■ Preservation method	■ Replacement parts availability
■ Packaging procedure	■ Vintage	■ Energy source
■ Minimum weight per case	■ Alcohol content	■ Excess capacity
■ Product yield	■ Lifetime cost	■ Add-on capabilities
■ Point of origin	■ Potential operating savings	■ Warranty
■ Product form	■ Direct purchase	■ Code compliance
■ Color	■ Demonstration models	■ Service plans
■ Degree of ripeness	■ Equipment programs	■ Quality
■ Ripening process used	■ Custom fee	■ Vendor reputation
■ Preservation method	■ New vs. used FF&E	

Activity

Selecting FF&E Criteria

Reviewing the selection factors in *Exhibit 4c*, list in the space below the criteria that you would include on a product specification for a dishwasher (FF&E item) for a full-service operation.

_____

_____

_____

_____

_____

_____

_____

_____

_____

Step 3: Define Ordering Procedures

After a goods and services needs assessment has been completed and products have been selected that reflect the operation's quality standards, the next step in the procurement process is ordering products.

Ordering procedures may vary based on the size of the operation. It is usual for "mom and pop" shops to simply place orders by phone with an approved supplier, whereas larger operations have more formal procedures. Additionally, the paperwork for ordering products varies from operation to operation.

In some establishments, as indicated in Step 1, the buyer assesses the needs of different departments and the frequency of which these needs must be fulfilled. In these instances, the buyer takes care of inventory for the department without the department's input. Other establishments, usually larger ones, dictate that department managers (such as chefs or bar managers) submit **purchase requisitions,** which detail their department's product needs to the purchaser before the order is placed. Purchase requisitions are also used for irregular purchases or for items that need to be bought independently of the usually scheduled order.

Controlling the sequence of activities in the procurement process is important. Many operations use a **purchase order,** which is a multipart form that stipulates what is wanted, when it is wanted, and what the product's AP cost is, as well as the terms of delivery, replacement, and returns, as shown in *Exhibit 4d*. For record-keeping purposes, copies of the completed form are distributed to different parties as listed on the bottom of the form.

Establishing a replacement and return policy is also important. There are instances when a supplier's distributed products do not meet the operation's quality standards and the paid deposit needs to be reimbursed. The terms of how that is done ideally should be discussed with the supplier prior to ordering.

No matter the formality of the operation's ordering procedure, after determining what to order, you must determine the correct order size. Once this is known, you can elect to place an order in several ways:

1. In person or by phone with the supplier's salesperson or **distributor sales representative (DSR)**

2. Faxing the order

3. Emailing the order

4. Ordering online

Management typically determines which ordering procedure is used, as well as the procedures for the receiving, storing, and issuing components of the procurement process.

Step 4: Define Receiving Procedures

"You don't always get what you pay for." This adage helps explain why receiving procedures are a component of the procurement process. Checking and either accepting or refusing deliveries is the main function of **receiving**.

Just as ordering procedures vary based on the size of the operation, so do receiving procedures. Some operations require internal staff to control this function, while others allow the delivery person access to storage facilities where he or she can remove unwanted items, restock, and leave the invoice with someone. Regardless of the specific steps involved, it is critical that the procedure be controlled. Several factors must be in place to guarantee that the receiving procedure is accurately performed. (See *Exhibit 4e* on p. 60.)

Many operations believe the process of inventory control begins once the products are accepted by the receiving staff because these products have been confirmed as having met the operation's quality standards and are subsequently distributed to the appropriate internal units.

Exhibit 4d

Sample Multipart Form Purchase Order

Operation's name: _____

Operation's address: _____

Purchase order number: _____ (Show this number on all orders)

Order date: _____

Transportation requirements: _____

Send order by: _____

Quantity Ordered	Size of Unit	Item Description	Unit Price	Total Price
			Subtotal	
			Tax	
			Shipping	
			Total	

If you cannot comply with these directives, please immediately notify the person below.

Returns policy: _____

For Use by Receiving Clerk

Received by: _____

Date received: _____

Condition of goods: _____

Other remarks: _____

Ordering party contact information: _____

Authorized signature: _____

ORIGINAL

VENDOR

RECEIVING

ACCOUNTING

Exhibit 4e

Receiving Basics

Suitable Receiving Dock/Service Area

The receiving area or dock should be clean, secure, well lit, and well located, so that it is practical for all relevant parties to deliver and receive goods and services.

Appropriate Receiving Equipment

Some products must be delivered at certain temperatures or weigh a certain amount. It is important that the receiving manager or personnel check both the product's quality—as shown in the photo on the right—and temperature to ensure that quality and food safety standards are met. Therefore, temperature probes, accurate scales, rule measures, and cutlery should be readily available for sampling and confirmation purposes. Calculators are also a basic necessity, as they verify that the costs on the purchase order are, in fact, the prices that were charged. Pallet jacks may also be needed to relocate inventory.

Capable Receiving Personnel

All receiving personnel must be appropriately trained to ensure that all products comply with the specified quality and safety standards. Though the cost of training may be considered pricey, the cost of storing and issuing defective products is far more expensive.

Receiving Schedule

Ideally, deliveries should be scheduled to allow time for the receiving clerk to ensure that a delivery meets quality and safety standards, and to appropriately distribute and store the delivery items prior to the arrival of subsequent deliveries. Ideally, products should not be received during rush hours. If this happens, quality and safety may be sacrificed.

Copy of Purchase Order

The purchase order can be used as a comparative measure against the supplier's invoice, which typically accompanies all deliveries and specifies what products were delivered and the quantity and cost of each of them. Checking the purchase order against the supplier's invoice confirms that the quality, quantity, and prices of the delivered products match what was ordered. If the order is delivered during down hours or when the establishment is closed, it is important that the receiving personnel check the ordered products immediately the next day. Some operations empower receiving personnel to resolve issues regarding quality and insufficient quantity directly with the supplier.

Copy of Product Specification

Supplying the receiving clerk with a copy of the product specification is most helpful, especially if the need for substitution(s) arises. The product spec serves as a quick and accurate substitution reference.

Step 5: Define Storing and Issuing Procedures

The same person who receives products typically stores and issues them in most operations, especially in smaller ones. For the sake of inventory control, most restaurant and foodservice operators agree that some separation of function is ideal. However, unless the operation is large with a high sales volume, most operations cannot justify the additional cost of labor, which may also include security staff to help control and guard against product loss as a result of theft or **pilferage,** also called inventory skimming or shrinkage. Those larger organizations that can support the additional labor cost sometimes separate the purchasing function from the receiving and storing function for this reason.

Products may also be lost due to **spoilage,** which occurs when a product becomes ruined and is no longer usable. Constructing appropriate environmental settings can greatly reduce spoilage. These settings include:

■ Adequate facility and storage space

■ Adherence to temperature requirements

■ Proper equipment and its maintenance

■ Storage facilities installed in close proximity to the production units and receiving area

■ **Storage area regulations,** which detail who can enter and remove items from the storage areas, and should be enforced.

Adherence to strict sanitation practices, which are regulated in many states and local municipalities, is critical and is also a control against loss due to spoilage. Just as it is imperative that staff involved in the procurement process be trained and competent in managing this function, employees who perform receiving and storing duties must also be qualified.

Further care must be taken to distinguish among the issuing considerations for perishable versus nonperishable food products. FF&E are directly distributed to the departments that ordered them. Generally speaking, most perishable food, with the exception of meat and beverage alcohols, are typically issued directly to the requesting department, and nonperishable food and nonfood items are sent to a central storage facility and issued on an as-needed basis. Perishable food, such as the items in *Exhibit 4f* on the next page, deteriorates quickly, so handling it more than necessary may contribute to its deterioration.

Think About It...

Improper storage can cause a loss in a product's nutritional or taste value; however, the greatest consequence of improperly storing food is potential foodborne illness.

Exhibit 4f

Examples of perishable products

Issuing Considerations: Perishable Products

- **Fresh produce**—It is typical for these products to be received and issued directly to the production unit in the form in which they will be consumed or in **ready-to-go** form to minimize labor cost and preparation waste.

- **Dairy**—Like fresh produce, most dairy products spoil quickly and should be handled as little as possible. If dairy products are not used immediately upon receipt, they are usually issued to a central storage facility. It is important that they be issued according to expiration date, with older products being issued first.

- **Eggs**—Eggs should be issued and immediately refrigerated. They should be issued on an as-needed basis from either a central storage facility or the production unit's storage facility, as they rapidly deteriorate after leaving refrigeration.

- **Poultry**—Like other perishable food, poultry should be correctly rotated from stock.

- **Fish**—Not only does fish deteriorate rapidly, but it is also expensive. Fish is almost always issued directly to the production unit, where it can be immediately prepared or prepped and stored in the appropriate sections of the freezer. As fish is an expensive item, if the latter is the case, a stock requisition is typically needed to get it, especially in larger operations with a more formalized inventory control.

- **Meat**—In most operations, meat is added to a **perpetual inventory,** which is a record or theoretical count of the products placed into and taken from inventory that is "perpetually" updated at a central storage facility. A stock requisition is needed before a product is issued to the production unit. Meat is expensive; to avoid waste and pilferage, the chef or unit production manager should request and retrieve only the amount of meat needed for a current shift or event. If unused meat must be returned to the central storage facility at the shift's conclusion, it is important that it be properly located in the storage facility. The meat can only be returned if it was kept in time and temperature control. If it was time and temperature abused it must be discarded. Furthermore, it is critical that all meat is correctly rotated, and that the **in-process inventory**—which is the amount of inventory currently being used in production—and the perpetual inventory do not become too large.

- **Beverage alcohols**—Strict control over **beverage alcohols,** which include distilled spirits, wine, and beer, should be maintained at all times. While a perpetual inventory is kept, it is extremely common for a **physical inventory** or real product count to be regularly done on all beverage alcohols. Beverage alcohols can evaporate and develop offensive odors and flavors. Some can change composition, are sensitive to temperature, or cannot easily be preserved once opened (if at all). A few may be repurposed. Regardless, it is imperative that some form of control be exercised prior to issuing any beverage alcohol. Some operations require requisitions; some code or mark the bottles as safeguards against theft. There are countless opportunities for dishonesty in the bar business. The primary consideration, therefore, must be tight supervision and control relative to beverage alcohol issuance.

Issuing Considerations: Nonperishable and Nonfood Products

While nonperishable products like those in *Exhibit 4g*, have a much longer **shelf life,** or preservation period, than perishable products, more control over issuing them is necessary because they are typically stored in a central storage facility upon receipt as opposed to the production unit. Storage area regulations should be enforced for these types of items to minimize the risk of loss due to pilferage or waste.

Issuing Considerations: FF&E

Upon inspection and acceptance, it is a very common practice to issue FF&E, like those in *Exhibit 4h*, directly to the intended area of use. Due to their typically large expense, these items require requisitions.

Exhibit 4g

Examples of nonperishable products

Exhibit 4h

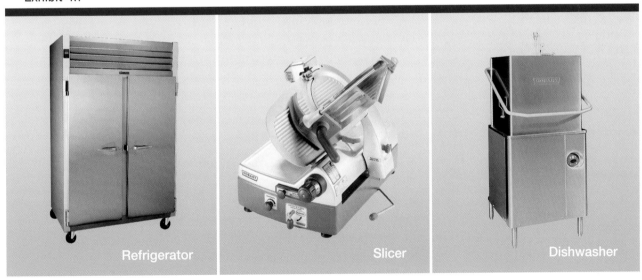

Refrigerator Slicer Dishwasher

FF&E products

Courtesy of Hobart Corporation

Supplier Selection

No matter how outstanding an operation's procurement process is, if the suppliers are unsatisfactory, it will make little difference. Likewise, a supplier may elect not to work with a particular operation because it cannot, or will not, work under the guidelines of that operation's buying plan or procurement policy. Those with purchasing responsibility should seek suppliers who are considered to be ethical, reliable, and financially stable or are deemed to be part of the **approved supplier list.** An approved supplier list is a list of suppliers created by the organization that have met the necessary criteria in regard to food safety, product quality, and price. In regard to food safety, the FDA defines "approved" as acceptable to the regulatory authority based on a determination of conformity with principles, practices, and generally recognized standards that protect public health. Two types of procurement policies are available to an operation:

- **"One-stop shop" buying plan**—When a purchaser chooses one or two supplier(s) to meet all of the operation's buying needs

- **Bid buying plan**—Allows for various suppliers to respond to a **request-for-bid** or **request-for-price (RFP),** asking them to (1) bid for the operation's business and (2) submit their prices for different goods and services based on the operation's product specifications

It is typical for smaller operations to adopt the one-stop shop buying plan and for larger operations to engage in a bid buying plan. However, an operation may choose to procure some of its products, like fresh produce or meat, from a specific supplier and other perishable or nonperishable items, nonfood items, or FF&E from the supplier whose bid is most acceptable. Notwithstanding, it is critical to realize that the lowest price does not always mean the best quality or lowest EP cost.

While product quality is primary, most purchasing managers initially factor in a supplier's reliability and the AP price of its products. In addition, purchasing managers examine other selection variables that are pertinent to their operation's mission and goals and meet its quality standards. From there, they begin to whittle down the initial list of potential suppliers.

Supplier Selection Criteria

When considering suppliers, take an exhaustive look at them. In some instances vendors outsource the supply of certain products to another vendor, or outsource their delivery to a third-party service. In either example, you have to make sure these additional parties meet your criteria and are going to supply you with the same desired results. Once a product is received at your operation, its quality cannot be increased or made better, it can only become worse. Thus, choosing a creditable and reliable supplier is key.

Here are points to verify when selecting vendors:

- Suppliers' facilities should be sanitary in regard to storage, handling, and delivery.

- Suppliers who supply meat, poultry, and egg products must be inspected by the USDA.

- Suppliers must be compliant with applicable local, state, and federal laws.

- Suppliers should be able to provide you with a list of references to prove they are reputable.

- Suppliers that are inspected must have a Hazard Analysis and Critical Control Point (HACCP) program in place.

- Suppliers that provide refrigerated storage or frozen products must have holding units that can maintain the products at the required internal temperature.

- Suppliers' delivery trucks must be able to maintain the required internal temperature of the product.

- Suppliers must have procedures in place to ensure their personnel are following proper personal hygiene practices.

Points to Review with the Supplier and Include in Contract

Once you select a supplier, put a contract in place. These are some points to review with the vendor and include in the contract:

- Ask the supplier to visit your establishment to take notes about anything that could make the delivery process difficult.

- Review the receiving area together, viewing the amount of space, exits, doors, etc.

- Discuss acceptable delivery times and days. Do not set yourself up for failure by allowing deliveries during busy mealtimes.

- Communicate your requirements for the drop-off area (e.g., how long a vendor's truck may be in an unrefrigerated area). You also need to know whether the vendor's truck is loaded in a refrigerated area. If not, the loading time adds additional exposure for the food to be time and temperature abused, which can make food unsafe.

- Specify in the contract who can accept a delivery.

- Be sure to communicate your standards to the vendor, in writing when possible.

No-Name or Independent Delivery Service

You need to be aware of whether or not a supplier has its own delivery service or whether this service is outsourced, particularly when selecting suppliers from a phone book or the Internet. E-suppliers have become very popular, but you must know the supplier as well as any of its subcontractors. It is a good idea for buyers to inspect the delivery vehicles or any intermediary storage facility associated with a delivery service.

References

You should routinely network with others in the foodservice industry to check out potential standard sources of suppliers. You might also receive referrals from trusted competitors or from national, state, or local restaurant associations in printed materials or from their Web sites. (See *Exhibit 4i.*)

Stockless Purchasing

When you suspect a pending increase in AP product costs or you have limited storage space, you may enter a purchasing arrangement known as **stockless purchasing**, which enables you to purchase a large quantity of a product at the current price, but directs the supplier to store it and deliver it as needed.

As a purchaser, you might want to consider this option when you order personalized items from a supplier that have your brand on them, such as china, tablecloths, napkins, etc. In this instance, you might be making this purchase because the price is going up and you do not want to incur an increase, and/or you know these items will need replacing in the future and you want to purchase them now. Either way, you can take advantage of the supplier storing certain items until you need them.

Exhibit 4i

Successful purchasers network with others in the industry.

Cost-Plus Purchasing

Cost-plus purchasing is an arrangement between a buyer and seller in which the supplier sells the products at cost, plus an agreed-upon supplier profit markup. Cost-plus purchasing demands that suppliers adjust their AP prices and share cost information, and therefore, many suppliers do not participate in this arrangement.

Standing Orders

Route salespeople are delivery staff who repeatedly deliver, assess inventory, and then stock an operation's supply of goods with an amount that would bring it up to **par,** or a fully stocked point. You might have standing orders for items that are routinely and predictably used such as bread, ice cream, or milk; however, you must be aware that having a route salesperson fill standing orders may challenge security controls. This type of relationship does not usually occur until you have built trust with the supplier.

Credit Terms

How credit terms are handled is important when identifying the ideal supplier. The amount and type of discounts, the interest charges, credit period, and billing procedures that a supplier offers are all critical considerations. Purchasers tend to seek suppliers who offer superior terms of credit. For large organizations with volume purchases, generous credit terms are one of the defining factors in supplier selection.

Return and Replacement Policy

When considering an ideal supplier, buyers must discuss the terms associated with product replacement and returns, as well as the reimbursement of any monetary deposit made for goods that need to be returned or are no longer wanted.

Selecting the Ideal Supplier

Supplier selection criteria may vary from operation to operation. With an awareness of sales strategies and emphasizing the importance of relationship building, most purchasers carefully reflect on the criteria prior to selecting a supplier.

Ultimately, you want to consider and regard your ideal supplier as you would an employee. If the supplier has proven to be a central component of the operation, you may make the supplier a house account, for example. If the supplier does not perform to expectation, you might take some form of corrective or disciplinary action—the most severe one would be ending the relationship with the supplier.

In any case, be prudent when determining the operation's buying plan and select a supplier who can fully accommodate it. Equally important, a supplier should act in your operation's best interests.

It is a good practice to evaluate the performance of your suppliers once a year. Throughout the year document issues that arise and how the supplier resolved them. At the yearly review, determine whether the service, quality of products, and prices fulfilled your standards. Meet with the suppliers and review any issues. If you decide to renew your contract, review it again before signing it, and ensure that all of your concerns and issues have been addressed.

Activity

Procurement Policy Dilemma

Robert and Marilyn Heyburn have just opened their first operation. They are the proud owners/managers of Robmar's Family Restaurant, where Marilyn is also the chef and Robert is the host.

The Heyburns intend to buy the majority of their products from one supplier who offers the following services to any of its customers: delivery, removal, and restocking of all products.

Given their busy roles, Robert and Marilyn are uncertain as to whether they should allow their supplier's delivery person access to their operation's storage areas, and whether they should also give this individual total control over their operation's receiving and storing functions, or just some control for items with a low unit cost, such as bread.

Consider their situation and list the advantages and disadvantages of each option.

Summary

While there are many considerations in the procurement and supplier selection process, an operation's mission, goals, and quality standards are the foundation on which all else is built. Buyers and suppliers are an integral part of any restaurant or foodservice operation. Selecting the optimal buying plan and supplier is paramount. You can select a supplier first and then work together to meet your needs, or you can create specifications for the needed products and request bids from potential suppliers.

Purchasing perishable and nonperishable food products, nonfood products, FF&E, and services requires that purchasers, unit managers, chefs, and inventory and receiving clerks, as well as suppliers and distributors, be trained and reliable relative to their role(s) in the procurement process. Ultimately, you need to be prudent and thorough when determining the operation's buying plan and selecting a supplier who can fully accommodate it.

Review Your Learning

1 Which perishable food is *not* directly issued to the production unit?

A. Dairy

B. Meat

C. Eggs

D. Produce

2 Nonperishable food products include

A. value-added products.

B. meat and fish.

C. some produce.

D. beer.

3 Purchasers always want to consider and regard a supplier as a

A. creditor.

B. friend.

C. trusted employee.

D. permanent stakeholder.

4 When initially choosing a supplier, you should consider

A. the quality of the supplier's products.

B. the supplier's facility.

C. credit terms.

D. whittling down the list of potential suppliers.

5 The person who receives products typically

A. pilfers them.

B. stores and issues them.

C. does not check for quality.

D. selects the suppliers.

6 A goods and services needs assessment is done

A. twice per year.

B. as a safeguard against pilferage and theft.

C. to determine what the operation has versus what it needs.

D. more often in larger operations than in smaller operations.

7 List the standard sources of suppliers.

_____

_____

_____

_____

8 Identify and briefly describe two basic buying plans.

_____

_____

_____

_____

9 Define perpetual inventory.

_____

_____

_____

_____

10 Define physical inventory.

_____

_____

_____

_____

Inventory Control

Inside This Chapter

- Managing Inventory to Volume
- Optimal Inventory Level
- Inventory Control and Management Systems

After completing this chapter, you should be able to:

- Calculate correct order quantities.
- Estimate appropriate timing of orders.
- Explain perpetual and physical inventory systems.

Test Your Knowledge

1 **True or False:** The main objective of inventory management is to have an overabundance of inventory. *(See p. 75.)*

2 **True or False:** Par stock is the amount of inventory needed to maintain a continuing supply of items from one delivery to the next. *(See p. 76.)*

3 **True or False:** Buyers typically accept the supplier's stipulated ordering procedures and delivery schedules when determining the correct order size and timing for their operation's items. *(See pp. 76–77.)*

4 **True or False:** Small operations typically do no more than is necessary to manage their storage areas. *(See p. 84.)*

5 **True or False:** A perpetual inventory is an actual valuing and counting of the items in storage, including—in some cases—those in the in-process inventory. *(See p. 84.)*

Key Terms

As purchased (AP) price

Bin card

Capital cost

Carrying cost

Customer count forecast

Economic order quantity (EOQ)

Edible portion (EP) cost

EP per product unit

EP per serving

Forecasted usage/supply of a particular item for this period

Historical usage data

In-process inventory

Inventory turnover

"Just in time" (JIT) inventory management

Levinson method

Management information system (MIS)

Menu price

Opportunity cost

Order size

Par stock approach

Percentage of sales volume

Perpetual inventory management

Perpetual inventory system

Physical inventory management

Popularity index

Portion divider (PD)

Portion factor (PF)

Reorder point (ROP)

Standard cost

Standard serving cost

Storage cost

Total annual costs

Introduction

Inventory control systems are essential for monitoring product quantities. Ideally, foodservice establishments strive to keep on hand only the needed quantity of food and nonfood products to meet customer needs—without experiencing stock outs—but not more inventory than needed in order to avoid the risk of increased loss.

Managing inventory varies among establishments. While some give it more attention than others, managing inventory is nevertheless important for operations to organize and control their inventories to meet this ideal.

Evaluating product usage rates, food costs, storage and ordering costs, as well as loss due to spoilage, pilferage, theft, or obsolescence, assists purchasers and inventory managers in developing cost-effective inventory management procedures.

Managing Inventory to Volume

The most important components of inventory management are knowing what quantity of product to order and when to order it. Without this information, the optimal level of food and nonfood products cannot be maintained.

In an effort to manage inventory to the anticipated sales volume, purchasers use various input to determine as correctly as possible the optimal inventory amount in relation to anticipated customer consumption.

Inventory Turnover

Purchasers consider product turnover when managing inventory to the anticipated volume. **Inventory turnover** in the restaurant industry is the time it takes for the inventory to move from the operation's receiving docks to the table to be consumed by customers. The operation's inventory management plan or ordering procedure should reflect the product turnover rate of the establishment. While there is no universally accepted level of inventory turnover, most operations predict that food inventory turns over approximately 20 times per year and liquor inventory turns over about 8.5 times per year.

Percentage of Sales Volume

Purchasers also consider the **percentage of sales volume** estimate to determine what amount of inventory should be available in stock to meet the operation's expected level of sales. There are diverse rules of thumb regarding the proper amount of inventory that should be available at any given point in time. It is typical for a full-service operation to have food, nonfood, and beverage products in inventory that are equal in dollar amount to no more than 1 percent of its annual sales volume. So if the operation's sales volume is two million dollars, it should not have products in inventory equal in dollar value to more than twenty thousand dollars, which is 1 percent of its sales volume.

A related rule-of-thumb offers that inventory should not be more than approximately one-third of the average monthly product costs.

Optimal Inventory Level

Both inventory turnover and percentage of sales provide excellent rules of thumb regarding an appropriate dollar value of inventory. However, they do not provide enough information on which to base orders for specific products. Knowing product usage, inventory costs, and food costs will help you determine the optimal inventory amount or what to order and when.

Product Usage

Two approaches are typically considered when calculating optimal inventory amounts:

- Par stock (a widespread approach)

- The Levinson method (a plan considered more complicated, but becoming increasingly used)

In both the par stock and Levinson methods, a necessary first step is to calculate your operation's expected usage of food, nonfood, and beverage items for the upcoming period.

Calculating Usage

To properly calculate expected usage, you will use historical usage data as a starting point. As discussed in Chapter 1, **historical usage data** is comprised of customer count histories, the item's popularity index, and an analysis of outside influences that might affect usage such as conventions, festivals, and weather forecasts. This information is considered when determining optimal order amounts. It is important to keep in mind that while usage patterns are variable, buyers must seek to determine a usage pattern based on this data.

For example, you would like to calculate the usage for boneless, six-ounce chicken breast in order to determine the amount of this item you need for the upcoming period. You know the following historical data: guest count last period was 5,200 people, the expected percentage increase in guest count for next period is 2 percent, and 2,111 customers ordered boneless, six-ounce chicken breast last period.

The **customer count forecast,** or number of customers expected in the upcoming period, can be calculated using one of these formulas:

$$\text{Customer count last period} + \left(\text{Customer count last period} \times \text{\% increase expected} \right) = \text{Customer count forecast this period}$$

$$\text{Customer count last period} - \left(\text{Customer count last period} \times \text{\% decrease expected} \right) = \text{Customer count forecast this period}$$

In this section's example, the operation expects an increase, so the first formula is used.

5,200 + (5,200 × 2%) = 5,304

5,200 + 104 = 5,304

Of the 5,304 customers expected in the next period, how many are likely to order boneless, six-ounce chicken breast? By determining the popularity index for the item and applying it to the forecasted customer count, you will be able to answer this question. The popularity index, also known as the menu mix percentage, is determined by dividing the number of customers who selected this item by the total number of customers.

$$\text{Number of customers choosing a particular entrée} \div \text{Total number of entrées sold} = \text{Popularity index of a particular entrée}$$

2,111 ÷ 5,200 = .41

The forecasted usage (of boneless, six-ounce chicken breasts needed) for this period is found by multiplying the forecast customer count by the popularity index as shown in the calculation below:

$$\text{Customer count forecast for this period} \times \text{Popularity index of a particular item} = \text{Forecasted supply of a particular item for this period}$$

5,304 × .41 = 2,174.64 or ≈ 2,175

Therefore, 2,175 boneless, six-ounce chicken breasts will be required to comply with your operation's usage pattern for the upcoming period.

Although you have calculated the number of chicken breasts your operation will likely need for the next period, your actual order size and order timing will depend on whether your operation uses the par stock approach or the Levinson approach to determine and maintain an optimal inventory level.

Activity

Part One: Forecast Usage

Sally is the buyer for Preston's Restaurant. She is purchasing the food items that make up the twelve-ounce filet mignon meal that is served with carrots and corn. Sally knows that Preston's typically serves three thousand customers per week and that 20 percent of weekly customers historically order the twelve-ounce filet mignon meal. Preston's does not expect an increase or decrease in customer counts for next week. What will the forecasted usage be for the twelve-ounce filet mignon meal?

Par Stock Approach

Many operations use the **par stock approach,** which requires that the purchaser determine the level of inventory items that must continually be in stock from one delivery date to the next to meet consumer demand. This is a simple approach that consists of these steps:

1 Accept the selected supplier's ordering process and delivery schedules. Purchasers typically cannot alter a selected supplier's schedule without incurring costs, such as increased delivery charges; this is why they follow the supplier's schedule.

2 Determine the par stock level for all inventory items. In order to make this determination, consider sales projections based on historical usage data. Keeping in mind that ordering dates will likely precede delivery dates by an amount of time, you must decide in advance when to order the appropriate amount of each item to maintain its par level. For example, the selected supplier's schedule may dictate that expensive perishable items, such as meat, be delivered only a few times each week. Given this, you would likely set the par stock for meat so that it lasts three or four days. Conversely, if the item is nonperishable and inexpensive like paper products, you may set a larger par stock, especially if there is enough storage space available.

3 Calculate the order quantity by subtracting what is currently in stock from par stock. Before placing orders, also consider whether to order more of each item based on seasonal changes, conventions, banquets, safety reserves, or other similar reasons.

Consider this example: you need eleven cases of canned mixed vegetables in stock to last from one order to the next. You place orders for this item every Tuesday morning and receive a delivery of it the next day. Just before ordering, you determine that there are two cases of mixed vegetables in stock, one of which will be used that day. You also know that between orders the operation will have a banquet, in which five additional cases will be used.

Think About It...

BUYERS BEWARE:
Inventory may exceed anticipated volume when financial incentives to buy large product quantities exist.

Therefore, given that the par stock is eleven, you subtract what will be on hand the day of delivery, which is one case, from the par stock of eleven, and then add five more cases for the banquet ($[11 - 1] + 5 = 15$) and calculate that fifteen cases need to be ordered.

No matter the product mix, it is important that you set par stock levels for all inventory items relative to the supplier's ordering and delivery terms such that the amount of item lasts between planned deliveries. Par stocks should be reevaluated from time to time or if the supplier's delivery schedule changes or the buyer changes suppliers.

This approach to calculating and ordering product quantities works very well, given that it is very simple, deliveries are predictable, and that it is fairly uncommon for the operation to change its menu offerings. However, because the par stock approach exclusively focuses on establishing and maintaining product par level, it does not greatly consider food costs or the costs of ordering or storing food.

Levinson Method

While similar to the par stock approach, the **Levinson method** more precisely forecasts the amount of product to order based on each item's consumed portion size relative to that item's sales volume for a specific period.

This method is gaining popularity because the foodservice industry is becoming computerized. Therefore, data are available that allow purchasing managers to more easily calculate food cost information, as shown in the following steps:

1. Accept the supplier's ordering procedures and delivery schedule.

2. Determine the par stock level for all inventory items. Knowing that ordering dates will likely precede delivery dates by an amount of time, decide when it would be best to order the appropriate amount of each item to maintain its par level.

3. Forecast the amount of each item needed to meet sales volume based on historical data or usage information.

   A. For example, earlier in this chapter you calculated that approximately 2,175 boneless, six-ounce chicken breasts would be needed for the next period.

   B. Determine the raw pounds (or appropriate unit of measurement) of each ingredient needed to meet the forecast. This is done by determining the **portion factor (PF)** and **portion divider (PD)** for each item.

The **portion factor** is the number of portions available in one pound (or other appropriate measure) as calculated below:

$$\begin{array}{c}\textbf{16 oz.} \\ \textbf{(if raw pounds is the} \\ \textbf{unit of measurement)} \end{array} \div \begin{array}{c} \textbf{Amount of an} \\ \textbf{ingredient needed} \\ \textbf{for one serving} \end{array} = \begin{array}{c} \textbf{Portion} \\ \textbf{factor} \end{array}$$

For the boneless, six-ounce chicken breasts the portion factor is 2.67.

16 ÷ 6 = 2.67

The portion divider is the number of portions available in one pound (or other appropriate measure) after the item's edible yield is taken into account.

PF × Ingredients edible yield percentage = PD

For the boneless, six-ounce chicken breasts, the portion divider is calculated as below:

2.67 × 80% = 2.14

The edible yield percentage is most often determined by the supplier and is accepted by you. However, you can compute the edible yield percentage by assessing each item's average necessary waste and then shopping around for a new supplier who offers a yield percentage that is more reflective of the operation's production.

ⓒ Once the PF and PD are computed, determine each item's order size.

Number of customers
who will consume the **÷ Ingredient's PD = Order size**
ingredient (item's usage)

Given that 2,175 customers are forecasted to eat the boneless, six-ounce chicken breast, you can calculate the correct order size for this item.

2,175 ÷ 2.14 = 1016.4 lb

Think About It...

Large orders translate into increased storage costs and decreased ordering costs; small orders translate into decreased storage costs and increased ordering costs.

Activity

Part Two: Calculate Portion Factor, Portion Divider, and Order Size

Sally is using the Levinson method to compute the order quantities for the twelve-ounce filet mignon meal with corn and carrots. She knows the serving size and edible yield percentage of each item in the filet mignon meal. Calculate the portion factor and portion divider. Using your answer from Part One of this activity on p. 76, calculate the order size in raw pounds for each item.

Ingredient	Serving Size	Edible Yield	PF	PD	Order Size
Steak	12 oz	85%			
Corn	5 oz	95%			
Carrots	4 oz	90%			

Activity

Frank–n–Stein's Product Order

Frank Koenig is the owner/chef of "Frank-n-Stein's," a local bratwurst and beer establishment. He has a limited menu at his very solid and predictable business. Long ago he determined that he needs enough product to serve 1,675 customers every week. Frank recently decided to hire you as an assistant chef/buyer to help him.

Frank places orders on Monday and Thursday. It is time to place Monday's order, which includes four items out of his product mix. Given the following data, Frank would like you to compute the correct order size needed to serve his weekly customer count for these items:

1. **Liters of beer** (the numerator of your PF equation is 1,000 ml): Serving size— 60 ml; Servable yield percentage—95 percent

   _____

2. **Gallons of mustard** (the numerator of your PF equation is 128 oz): Serving size ¼ oz; Edible yield percentage—98 percent

   _____

3. **Pounds of bratwurst** (the numerator of your PF equation is 16 oz): Serving size—13 oz; Edible yield percentage—85 percent

   _____

4. **Cases of onions** (the numerator of your PF equation is 16 oz): Serving size—2 oz; Edible yield percentage—75 percent; Minimum weight per case—54 lb

   _____

Inventory Costs

Using either one or a combination of the par stock approach or Levinson method to calculate the correct order quantities would be incomplete without considering other pertinent variables related to optimal order amount. The costs associated with ordering and storing inventory also influence the correct order timing and size.

The cost of insurance, the maintenance cost of the storage facility, as well as the costs associated with spoilage and outdated or expired items are a few of the factors that help define **storage cost**. Storage cost, also known as the product's **carrying cost**, is the sum of all costs associated with properly storing food, beverage, and nonfood items from the time they are received from the supplier until they are used. Arguably, the greatest facet of the inventory's storage cost is the **opportunity cost** or **capital cost**, which indicates how much of the operation's money is invested in its inventory and, as a result, cannot be used for any other purpose.

While the estimated costs of placing an order vary, it is fiscally prudent for the buyer to minimize the number of orders that need to be placed because placing orders is not free.

The buyer must consider both the storage and ordering costs when calculating the correct order size and time. The **economic order quantity (EOQ)** is the most cost effective quantity to order. It offers a clearer point of view on how storage and ordering costs impact the optimal order size and time; the calculation for EOQ is illustrated below. It can be calculated in two ways, EOQ in dollars and EOQ in number of units.

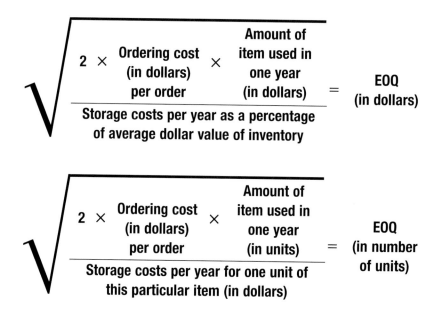

$$\sqrt{\frac{2 \times \begin{array}{c}\text{Ordering cost} \\ \text{(in dollars)} \\ \text{per order}\end{array} \times \begin{array}{c}\text{Amount of} \\ \text{item used in} \\ \text{one year} \\ \text{(in dollars)}\end{array}}{\begin{array}{c}\text{Storage costs per year as a percentage} \\ \text{of average dollar value of inventory}\end{array}}} = \begin{array}{c}\text{EOQ} \\ \text{(in dollars)}\end{array}$$

$$\sqrt{\frac{2 \times \begin{array}{c}\text{Ordering cost} \\ \text{(in dollars)} \\ \text{per order}\end{array} \times \begin{array}{c}\text{Amount of} \\ \text{item used in} \\ \text{one year} \\ \text{(in units)}\end{array}}{\begin{array}{c}\text{Storage costs per year for one unit of} \\ \text{this particular item (in dollars)}\end{array}}} = \begin{array}{c}\text{EOQ} \\ \text{(in number} \\ \text{of units)}\end{array}$$

Based on prior calculations, you know that your operation will require 1,016.4 pounds of boneless chicken breasts to meet customer demand in the upcoming period. By determining the EOQ, you will be able to determine the optimum order size.

Historically, the operation uses 12,196.8 pounds of boneless chicken breasts annually. The cost of one pound is $2.50. Your supplier typically charges you $2.00 per order. Your cold storage costs for the boneless chicken breast is 15 percent of the value of the chicken.

$$\sqrt{2 \times \$2.00 \times (12{,}196.8 \times \$2.50)} \div .15 = \$901.36$$

$$\sqrt{2 \times \$2.00 \times 12{,}196.8} \div (2.50 \times .15) = \begin{array}{l} 360.7 \text{ or} \\ 361 \text{ lb} \end{array}$$

In addition to knowing the EOQ in dollars and units, management might also want to know the total annual ordering and storage costs associated with this EOQ of 361 pounds. You can calculate this information by using the calculation below.

$$\frac{\text{Ordering cost per order} \times \text{Number of units used in one year}}{\text{Order size (in units)}} + \frac{\text{Storage cost per year of one unit} \times \text{Order size (in units)}}{2} = \text{Total annual costs}$$

$$\frac{\$2.00 \times 12{,}196.8 \text{ lb}}{361 \text{ lb}} + \frac{\$2.50 \times .15 \times 361 \text{ lb}}{2} = \text{Total annual costs}$$

$$\$67.57 + \$67.69 = \$135.26$$

Activity

Part Three: EOQ

Sally wants to calculate the EOQ of canned corn. Historically, Preston's has used three hundred cases of canned corn per year; some of that corn is an item in the twelve-ounce filet mignon meal. The cost of one case is $4.00, the ordering cost per order is $2.00, and the storage cost is 10 percent of the value of the corn.

1 What is the EOQ in dollars? _____

2 What is the EOQ in units?_____

Though you have considered all costs and given management the optimal order size, management may conclude that it is or is not desirable to order the EOQ of 361 pounds of boneless chicken breasts at one time. Nevertheless, knowing the EOQ and total annual costs of products can help the purchaser make informed decisions regarding the correct order sizes and timing.

Knowing this information, which allows you to keep total costs as low as possible and greatly minimize the risk of stock outs, allows you to better determine the reorder point (ROP) for an item. The **reorder point (ROP)** is the number of units to which the on-hand quantity should decrease before placing additional orders. In the case of the boneless chicken breasts, the buyer has determined that the ROP is 225 pounds. Many purchasers who compute the EOQ for their operation's product typically practice **"just in time" (JIT) inventory management**, in which items are ordered and received just in time to use them in the operation. This practice allows purchasers to maintain the most desirable inventory level at all times.

Activity

Part Four: Total Annual Costs

Management at Preston's has asked Sally to calculate the total annual costs for the canned corn. Use the EOQ in units you calculated in Part Three of the activity as your order size in units. Keep in mind that the ordering cost per order is $2.00; the cost per case of canned corn is $4.00.

1 What are the total annual costs for canned corn? _____

Food Costs

No matter the size of the foodservice establishment, or whether it requires that its products' EOQ be calculated, most operators and their purchasers are very concerned with every product's edible portion or EP cost.

Determining the EP price or food cost will help you assess whether an item's PD and PF should be adjusted, which could cause the order amount to change. This computation also provides you with input as to whether you should shop around for suppliers who offer better yield percentages or AP prices.

The price you should consider when purchasing a product is its optional price. A product's **optional price** is comprised of the lowest possible **edible portion (EP) cost** and the value added by the product's quality and associated supplier services.

Employing the Levinson method also enables you to easily calculate the EP food cost of each item on either a whole product unit or on a per-serving basis. After having computed the optimal order size and time, you have the required data to make these calculations. The only additional factor that needs to be included in these food cost equations is the product's **as purchased (AP) price,** which is readily available to you. Each supplier being considered by the operation during the initial stages of the supplier selection process provides it.

To calculate the product unit's EP cost, you need to know the product's AP price and edible yield percentage.

AP price ÷ Edible yield percentage = EP per product unit

To calculate the EP cost of a product on a per-serving basis—you need the item's AP price and PD (portion divider) that was already computed as part of the correct order size calculation.

Building on the boneless chicken breast example, compute the EP cost for each item on a product unit and per-serving basis.

AP price ÷ PD = EP per serving

Ingredient	AP price (per pound)	PD	Edible yield %
Chicken	$2.50	2.14	80%
EP computation per unit		**EP computation per serving**	
Chicken $2.50 ÷ 0.80 = $3.13		$2.50 ÷ 2.14 = $1.17	

Taking the EP per-serving cost one step further will provide the standard cost of a meal. For example, the boneless six-ounce chicken breasts (EP per-serving cost of $1.17) are used in a meal with rice pilaf (EP per-serving cost of $0.23) and carrots (EP per-serving cost of $0.11). The **standard serving cost** of this meal, which is the sum of all EP costs per serving, can be calculated as follows:

EP cost per serving (chicken) + EP cost per serving (rice) + EP cost per serving (carrots) = Standard cost (for boneless chicken breast meal)

Once the standard serving cost is known, production managers or chefs can set the menu costs of meals. For example, the production manager may determine that the standard cost of the chicken breast meal is 25 percent of its menu price.

$1.17 + $0.23 + $0.11 = $1.51

Standard cost ÷ Percentage of menu price = Menu price

Menu price computation for the chicken breast is then as follows:

$1.51 ÷ .25 = $6.04

The menu price of $6.04 is the recommended food cost to the customer. However, this may be adjusted to reflect competitive pricing or market conditions to a price that is more customer identifiable. A menu management course would illustrate various menu-pricing strategies.

An advantage of knowing the product's standard cost is that you or other managers consider it in the operation's overall inventory and cost-control management system.

Inventory Control and Management Systems

Inventory management is challenging for most foodservice operations because it costs a great deal of money and time; however, it is important that all operations manage their inventory for several reasons, including reducing the risk of loss.

While systematically managing all storage facilities is ideal, it is typical for small operations to do no more than is necessary to meet local legal conditions. It is more usual for larger operations to manage their inventory more tightly and systematically.

All operations must employ a systematic inventory management system relative to liquor control. Typically, state or local liquor commissions mandate that operations maintain accurate records of their liquor purchases. Many operations also administer some degree of control over expensive perishable items.

The foodservice industry typically uses one or both of the following systematic inventory management systems:

- **Perpetual inventory management**—record or theoretical count of the products placed into and taken from inventory that is "perpetually" updated

- **Physical inventory management**—actual valuing and counting of all current inventory including, at times, products that are being used in production or, in other words, are part of the **in-process inventory**

Perpetual Inventory

Many operations use stock requisitions when requesting and receiving liquor or expensive perishable items like meat, fish, and poultry.

A **perpetual inventory system** is a continuous record of items in inventory. The key advantage of "perpetually" updating the record for every item in an operation's inventory is information availability.

Many foodservice operators believe that unless their foodservice establishments have a **management information system (MIS)**, it is unreasonable to use a perpetual inventory system for more than a few products, like liquor or expensive perishable food items. It is becoming more common for larger operations to use a MIS.

If perpetual evidence for each product is kept, operators typically utilize a bin card to continually record changes and provide information relative to that item. A **bin card,** which is a record of when an item was delivered, when it was issued, to whom it was issued, and, in some cases, when it was returned to the storage facility is typically assigned and attached next to the item (on shelving, for example) in the storage area. (See *Exhibit 5a*.)

Exhibit 5a

Sample Bin Card

NAME OF ITEM Canned Corn							**BIN NUMBER** C 039		
Date delivered	**Unit price**	**No. of units delivered**	**Date issued**	**No. of units issued**	**Issued to**	**No. of units returned**	**Date returned**	**Balance**	
								180	
8/1								150	
			8/3	30	JL			50	
			8/3	100	RD			59	
						9	8/3	1379	
8/5		1320							

Physical Inventory

Instead of performing a perpetual inventory or relying on a speculative sum for each item in inventory, most operations take a physical inventory on a regular predetermined basis, such as every week, every two weeks, or every month. (See *Exhibit 5b* on the next page.)

Exhibit 5b

Taking physical inventory should be scheduled regularly.

Exhibit 5c

Monthly Actual Product Cost Example

BI + P − EI = C

$$\underset{\text{inventory}}{\text{Beginning}} + \underset{\text{for the month}}{\text{Purchases}} - \underset{\text{inventory}}{\text{Ending}} = \underset{\text{product cost}}{\text{Actual}}$$

For example:

Beginning inventory (BI) = $10,000

Purchases (P) = $43,000

Ending inventory (EI) = $9,000

Actual product cost (C) = $44,000

$$\underset{\text{(BI)}}{\$10{,}000} + \underset{\text{(P)}}{\$43{,}000} - \underset{\text{(EI)}}{\$9{,}000} = \underset{\text{(C)}}{\$44{,}000}$$

Though taking a physical inventory is time consuming, it must be done at minimum once per month in order for the monthly income statement to be prepared. This statement indicates the operation's cost of goods sold.

To ensure accuracy and engage a checks-and-balances system, some operation owners require that somebody other than the storeroom manager or purchaser perform the inventory.

No matter how the physical inventory is performed—or whether the product is counted by using a bar-code scanner or by manually counting—regularly valuing and counting items provides information that can be helpful to the operation in the ways listed below.

■ You need this information to know order quantities.

■ You need this information before you can prepare purchase orders.

■ If an operation does manage inventory using a perpetual inventory system, a comparative analysis between the actual physical inventory and the theoretical inventory can be made.

■ Actual product costs for a specific period of time—usually per month—can be calculated as shown in *Exhibit 5c.*

- Actual costs can be compared with standard costs; there should not be a great difference between these two costs.

- This information helps you reduce the risk of loss.

Inventory Loss

In spite of systematic inventory management systems, unless additional security measures are in place, the operation risks loss due to theft or pilferage. While theft and pilferage are not new to the foodservice industry, policies regarding these are changing due to raised awareness, the cost of insurance, and the increasing reluctance of operators to forward the costs of these losses to their customers in the form of elevated menu prices.

It has been estimated that the foodservice industry loses 3 to 8 percent of its gross sales due to internal theft and close to twenty billion dollars a year owing to theft and cash mishandling. Additionally, approximately 75 percent of all unaccounted inventory is due to theft, and the majority of employees who have pilfered or stolen products from their operations have worked there between five and seven years. (See *Exhibit 5d.*)

Not only must an operation hire honest purchasers and suppliers, but all other internal employees must also be trustworthy. Additionally, designing storage areas so that stringent security measures are possible and adhering to strict physical inventory management procedures can help minimize loss. Some operations separate the buying, receiving, storing, and issuing activities to minimize opportunities for theft or pilferage.

Other actions management can take in an effort to eliminate loss include these cost-effective physical barriers:

- Installing time locks or heavy-duty locks

- Disallowing loitering near the receiving and storage areas

- Ensuring that accounts are credited properly

- Marking invoices that are paid as "paid"

- Comparing invoices with purchase orders

- Employing "shoppers" or "spotters" in the front of the house

- Running integrity checks and drugs tests on all employees

- Disallowing employees from entering or leaving the premises via the dock door

Exhibit 5d

Loss-prevention techniques can help to minimize theft, or pilferage, by employees.

Summary

Calculating product usage, food storage, and ordering costs, as well as estimating product loss, is essential to calculating the optimum order size and time. These calculations are integral components of a systematic inventory control system.

While some operations use a perpetual inventory management system, most physically count and value their inventory on a regular basis. Two of the objectives of all operations relative to inventory management are (1) to keep only the needed quantity of food and nonfood products on hand to meet customer needs without experiencing stock outs, and (2) to *not* maintain more inventory than needed that could result in decreased profits and increased risk due to spoilage, obsolesce, pilferage, or theft.

Review Your Learning

1 If the beginning product inventory is $10,000, product purchases are $15,000, and the ending product inventory is $11,000, what is the actual food cost?

A. $14,000
B. $25,000
C. $21,000
D. $15,000

2 Perpetual inventory is

A. an actual counting and valuing of inventory.
B. a theoretical accumulating inventory.
C. an often used inventory control management method.
D. only done when all units are fully integrated with a MIS system.

3 When managing inventory to anticipated volume, buyers consider

A. taking an in-process inventory.
B. product turnover.
C. ordering less perishable products during unseasonable weather.
D. the supplier's terms.

4 It is useful to take a physical inventory for *all but which* reason?

A. Purchasers need this information to help them know order quantities.
B. Purchasers need this information before they can prepare purchase orders.
C. For an operation with a perpetual inventory system, purchasers can compare perpetual and actual inventory.
D. Purchasers do not have access to computer technology.

5 A bin card is used

A. when a bar code scanner is unavailable.
B. to prevent user error.
C. to record the item's receipt and issuance dates.
D. to decrease the time it takes to perform a physical inventory.

6 Whether the buyer uses the par stock approach or Levinson method when calculating optimal order amounts, what is the first thing he or she does?

_____

_____

_____

_____

_____

7 Given the following data, what is the number of raw pounds needed to serve 425 customers?

Ingredient: Flank steak

Serving size: 12 oz

Edible yield percentage: 85 percent

A. 376 lb
B. 17.7 lb
C. 17 lb
D. 37.6 lb

continued on next page

Review Your Learning *continued from previous page*

8 Given the following data, compute the EP price for beef brisket.

AP price: $2.98 per pound

Edible yield percentage: 75 percent

A. $3.79

B. $3.97

C. $2.24

D. $2.23

9 The standard cost of the chicken and rice dinner is $3.47. The manager has determined that the standard cost of the chicken and rice dinner menu item is 33 percent of its menu price. What is the suggested menu price of this dinner item?

A. $5.51

B. $10.52

C. $4.62

D. $7.05

10 Given the following data, calculate the EOQ in dollars and units.

☐ Operation uses 500 cases of canned sweet potatoes per year.

☐ The cost of one case of sweet potatoes is $6.25.

☐ The ordering cost per order is $3.00.

☐ The storage cost is 15 percent of the value of the sweet potatoes.

A. EOQ in dollars = 345
EOQ in units = 56.6

B. EOQ in dollars = 354
EOQ in units = 71.94

C. EOQ in dollars = 345
EOQ in units = 71.94

D. EOQ in dollars = 354
EOQ in units = 56.8

Field Project

Choosing the Right Produce

This field research project is designed to provide you with an opportunity to learn from practitioners in the restaurant and foodservice industry who obtain products and services for their operation. It will also ask you to research concepts and practices that have been introduced in this competency guide.

Assignment

While a purchaser may compare certain individual factors that appear to favor one supplier over another, the decision to select a supplier often requires the purchaser to look collectively at many factors. For example, an operation's fresh produce needs could be met by any number of supplier sources that vie for its business. To make the best choice, however, the purchaser must consider who can best support the operation's fresh produce needs and quality standards, while providing it with the best overall value. There are several alternatives for purchasing fresh produce. As a purchaser, you may choose to procure the fresh produce for your operation from an independent farmer, a fresh produce supplier, or a garden located on the operation's premise.

Your task for this project is to choose a supplier of produce for an operation of your choice. You will compare various qualities between two suppliers and determine which supplier source better satisfies the operation's produce requirements. At least ten items of produce must be considered for the comparison.

The report of your findings and the final recommendation should include:

■ Descriptions of the two supplier sources

■ Description of the restaurant or foodservice operation, including its concept and goals

■ Comparison of the suppliers' as purchased (AP) prices, quality, and supplier services for the same products and supplier services

■ Definition of what your operation means by quality, including AP prices, supplier services, federal government grades, packers' brands, brand names, etc.

■ Any other pertinent buyer/operational considerations that factor into this conclusion, such as:

  ☐ Operation's concept and goals

  ☐ Operation's menu

  ☐ Operation's budget

  ☐ Operation's selection and procurement policies (limiting quantities and prices, ethics code, etc.)

  ☐ Products' EP price

  ☐ Operation's supplier selection criteria

  ☐ Other pertinent product selection factors: product yield, product form, degree of ripeness, point of origin, preservation method, packaging procedure, etc.

  ☐ Operation's storage facilities

  ☐ Product availability (Is the desired product quality available? Can you get it when you need it?)

continued on next page

Choosing the Right Produce *continued from previous page*

☐ Reliability (product quality and supplier source consistency)

☐ Receiving practices (more or less controlled; who is responsible?)

☐ Operation's storage considerations

☐ Inventory control

☐ Par stock level

☐ Fresh produce handling (who and how often)

☐ Operation's issuing practices

☐ Season of the year

☐ Unexpected need or stock out

☐ Other factors pertinent to the operation

■ Rationale for choosing the supplier you did, including the advantages and disadvantages, as well as the efficiencies and deficiencies, of procuring fresh produce from each source.

Prework

In order to complete this assignment, you must complete these tasks first:

1 Identify an operation—it can be a chain or an independent restaurant or foodservice operation.*

2 Request permission to speak with the buyer of fresh produce for the operation.*

3 Research and understand the basic procurement process for fresh produce and the specifics of how it is purchased for your operation.

4 Identify what is included on a product specification sheet, as well as what information is included in general and for your operation.

5 Identify the inventory control policies and practices at your organization as they pertain to fresh produce.

6 Investigate supplier selection practices at your operation.

*If you are unable to identify an operation or secure permission to speak with a buyer, ask your instructor for assistance.